Negev
&
Southern Israel
Biblical Sites
Guide

Negev

&

Southern Israel

Biblical Sites Guide

Todd M. Fink

Negev

&
Southern Israel

Biblical Sites Guide
by
Todd M. Fink

Published by Selah Book Press

Cover Illustration Copyright © 2021 by Selah Book Press
Cover design by Selah Book Press

Copyright © 2021 by Todd M. Fink

ISBN-13: 978-1-944601-42-3

Second Edition

All rights reserved. No part of this publication may be reproduced or transmitted in any form or by any means, electronic or mechanical, including photocopy, recording, or any information storage retrieval system, without permission in writing from the copyright owner.

Scripture References are taken from the following Bible versions:

New American Standard Bible®,
Copyright © 1960, 1962, 1963, 1968, 1971, 1972, 1973,
1975, 1977, 1995 by The Lockman Foundation
Used by permission. (www.Lockman.org)

The Holy Bible, English Standard Version® (ESV®)
Copyright © 2001 by Crossway,
a publishing ministry of Good News Publishers.
All rights reserved.
ESV Text Edition: 2007

The Holy Bible, New International Version®, NIV® Copyright © 1973, 1978,
1984, 2011 by Biblica, Inc.® Used by permission. All rights reserved
worldwide.

The Holy Bible, New King James Version®. Copyright © 1982 by Thomas
Nelson, Inc. All rights reserved.

The NET Bible®, New English Translation (NET) Scripture quoted by
permission. Quotations designated (NET) are from the NET Bible® copyright
©1996-2006 by Biblical Studies Press, L.L.C.

Scripture in bold is emphasis added by the author.

Table of Contents

Acknowledgments 1

Israel: Land of the Bible 2

Negev & Southern Israel Sites 4

Tel Arad 5

Tel Beersheba 13

Bethlehem Overview 19

Bethlehem: Church of the Nativity 25

Bethlehem: Herodian Fortress 32

Bethlehem: Shepherds' Field 39

Beth-Shemesh 45

En Gedi 52

Exodus, Red Sea, and Mount Sinai 56

Hebron 68

Inn of the Good Samaritan 74

Jericho 80

Jordan River: Baptismal Site of Jesus 90

Jordan River: Crossing into the Promised Land 103

Judean Wilderness 110

Kadesh Barnea 116

Lachish 124

Masada 132

Qumran and the Dead Sea Scrolls 139

Sodom and Gomorrah 146

St. George's Monastery 155

Timna Park: Tabernacle Replica 161

Valley of Elah 169

Other Sites in Southern Israel 176

Timeline of Israel 185

Maps of Israel 191

Twelve Tribes of Israel 192

Divided Kingdom 193

Regions of Israel 194

Israel Today 195

Travel Orientation 196

Understanding the Holy Sites in Israel 197

How to Get the Most Out of Your Holy Land Trip 200

Understanding Group Travel Dynamics 202

Travel Tips for Israel 204

Packing List 205

About the Author 208

Books by Todd M. Fink 209

Connect with Todd 210

Acknowledgments

First and foremost, God deserves all the credit and glory for this book. He gave the desire, resources, time, strength, perseverance, and the ability to write it.

Secondly, for some unexplainable reason, God has filled the hearts of my wife and I with a deep desire to help people see the context of where the Bible took place. Of course, we know this desire is none other than God's sovereign work and grace. It's been a rich joy to have a small part in working with God's grace to provide this book.

What you as a reader find useful in this book, please give the glory and credit to God. What you find that is not useful or to your liking, please place the blame on the author.

Thirdly, I would like to thank my lovely wife, Letsy, for doing much of the research on the secondary "Other Sites of Interest" at the end of each section of the book. Significant time and effort were spent investigating these places.

Lastly, I'd like to thank my son, Joel, for helping with formatting, layout, and proofreading. He was a real trooper, and his contribution was invaluable.

My prayer is that God might use this book in your life to deepen your faith, your understanding of who God is, and how He has used the land of Israel and its people to communicate His eternal message to the world.

Israel: Land of the Bible

The Bible is not a fairy tale written in an unknown time, in an unreal place, and with unreal people. On the contrary, the Bible was written in real-time, in a real place, and with real people. The better we understand the context of the time, place, and people of the Bible, the better we will understand the Bible itself. In other words, by understanding the **world of the Bible** better, we can understand the **words of the Bible** better.

For a person of faith whose beliefs are engrained in the Bible, there is no place on earth like the Holy Land. In this narrow strip of land that connects the three major continents of Africa, Asia, and Europe, God sovereignly placed the land of Israel. It lies on the crossroads of the world and has affected virtually every civilization on earth.

From its barren hills and fertile plains, a message went out from a tethered and worn prophet that still applies today: *". . . and many peoples shall come, and say, 'Come, let us go up to the Mountain of the Lord, to the House of the God of Jacob; that He may teach us His ways and that we may walk in His paths. For out of Zion will go forth the law, and the word of the Lord from Jerusalem'"* (Isaiah 2:3–4).

Located on a tiny land bridge between Africa and Asia, there were few travel options between the two continents except through Israel. Therefore, whoever wanted to trade between the two continents, or control the known world, had to conquer and control Israel. For this reason, there have been more wars and conflicts in Israel than in any other country on earth. God positioned Israel in this unique location so He could influence the world and be on "Center Stage." In so doing, God's message of who He is, and His message of salvation and hope, is reaching the entire world.

For nearly 2,000 years, pilgrims of faith have come from all over the world to visit and experience the Holy Land, the land of their spiritual heritage. With Bibles in hand, these pilgrims have walked where Jesus walked and prayed in the places He preached and prayed. For Christians, there is just simply no place like Israel. As we traverse and experience the Holy Land, the better we understand Israel's land, places, and people. This great privilege allows us to better understand God's message written to us on the holy pages of Scripture, and as a result, live lives that glorify and fulfill God's purpose for our existence.

Negev & Southern Israel Sites

Tel Arad

Location

1. Tel Arad is in the Negev about 16 miles (26 km.) east of Tel Beersheba, and 33 miles (54 km.) south of Jerusalem.
2. Tel Arad covers an area of about 100 acres (40 hectares) and is on the west side of Hwy. 80.
3. Although this part of the Negev receives little rain, Arad is strategically situated on ancient trade routes.

Historical Background

1. Tel Arad has two major settlement periods, a Canaanite and an Israelite period. The lower part of the tel is from the Canaanite period, and the upper fortress part is from the Israelite period.
2. The Canaanites were the original settlers of Arad and established a large city here around 3500 BC. It had an estimated population of approximately 2,500 residents.
3. Israel captured Arad in the conquest under Joshua. Later, in around 940 BC, an Israelite settlement was established here.
4. Because Tel Arad is so strategically located and important, it was destroyed and rebuilt 6 times from the 9th to the 6th centuries. It was most likely destroyed in 701 BC by the Assyrians and again by the Babylonians in 586 BC.
5. Over 100 pottery shards (ostraca) were discovered at Tel Arad dating to the 7th and 6th centuries BC. Two of these are of great value as they mention two people from priestly families in the Bible, "Pashhur" from Ezra 2:38, and "Meremoth" from Ezra 8:33.
6. Two other pottery shards found at Tel Arad have written on them the name Arad, which confirms the city's identity.

Negev & Southern Israel Biblical Sites Guide

Places of Interest

1. Canaanite City
   - City Walls
   - City Gate
   - Temple
   - Palace
   - City Well
   - Homes
2. Entrance to Tel Arad
3. Upper Parking – Easy access to the Fortress Mound.

4. Israelite Fortress at Tel Arad
   - Although there was a small settlement during the time of Solomon, it was during the divided kingdom period that a fortress was set up at Tel Arad. The fortress served to protect Judah's southern border against its enemies.
   - The southern area of Judah was dangerous, and the fortress at Arad was destroyed 6 times during the divided kingdom period.
   - One of the destructions of the fortress likely occurred during Hezekiah's reign when he rebelled against the Assyrian King,

Sennacherib, in 701 BC. Scripture recounts how all the fortified cities of Judah were destroyed at this time (2 Kings 18:13).

- The fortress was rebuilt but destroyed again as a result of Nebuchadnezzar's conquest of Judah in 586 BC.
- During the Hellenistic period of the 3rd to 2nd centuries BC, a tower was built in the center of the fortress compound. During the Persian, Hellenistic, and Roman periods, the tower was repaired and used as a military post. During the early Arab period, the structure served as an inn for caravans.
- The fortress was finally abandoned in the 10th century AD.
- Entrance Towers
- Outer Court

5. Israelite Temple at Tel Arad

Arad had a functioning temple during the time of the divided kingdom that was somewhat similar to the temple in Jerusalem.

The temple at Arad was forbidden by God because the Israelites were to worship at no other place but Jerusalem at that time (Deut. 12:5–6).

- Outer Courtyard
- Altar
- Holy Place – In Scripture, the holy place was a long rectangular room. At Arad, it's a wide and rectangular room.
- Altars of Incense
- Holy of Holies
- Dimensions of the Holy of Holies – In the tabernacle God ordered Moses to erect, the required dimensions of the Holy of Holies were to be 10 cubits by 10 cubits (15 ft., 9 m.) (Ex. 26:31–33). In Solomon's temple, the Holy of Holies measured 20 cubits by 20 cubits (30 ft., 9 m.) (1 Kings 6:16). When the second temple was rebuilt under Ezra, the measurements of the Holy of Holies of Solomon's temple were kept.

Holy of Holies at the temple in Tel Arad

- The Holy of Holies at Arad measures about 7 ft. by 7 ft. (2.13 m.), much smaller than the tabernacle of Moses and the First and Second Temples in Jerusalem.
- Standing Stones – There are two standing stones in the Holy of Holies. One represents Yahweh and the other, Asherah, a false female god. This shows the worship of false gods mixed with the worship of God. Clearly, this was strictly forbidden.
- According to archeological data, the temple in Arad was destroyed during King Josiah's reign in about 630 BC (2 Kings 23:4–20). It's possible, though, that King Hezekiah could have removed the temple under his reforms (2 Kings 18:22).
- Even though the worshipers at Arad were commanded to tear down the temple there, they refused to do so and covered it over with dirt instead.

Negev & Southern Israel Sites

Arad in the Bible

1. **The King of Arad attacked Israel while they were making their way toward the Promised Land.**

   Numbers 21:1–3: *When the Canaanite, the king of **Arad**, who lived in the Negeb, heard that Israel was coming by the way of Atharim, he fought against Israel, and took some of them captive. 2 And Israel vowed a vow to the Lord and said, "If you will indeed give this people into my hand, then I will devote their cities to destruction." 3 And the Lord heeded the voice of Israel and gave over the Canaanites, and they devoted them and their cities to destruction. So the name of the place was called Hormah.*

   Tel Arad

2. **After the confrontation with the king of Arad, the Israelites turned around and headed south toward the Red Sea instead of entering the Promised Land from the Negev region (Num. 21:4).**

3. **The area of Arad was given to the tribe of Simeon during the conquest of the land (Josh. 19:1–8).**

4. **The relatives of Moses' father-in-law (Kenites) also settled in the area around Arad.**

   Judges 1:16–17: *And the descendants of the Kenite, Moses' father-in-law, went up with the people of Judah from the city of palms into the wilderness of Judah, which lies in the Negeb near **Arad**, and they went and settled with the people. 17 And Judah went with Simeon his brother, and they defeated the Canaanites who inhabited Zephath and devoted it to destruction. So the name of the city was called Hormah.*

Josiah's Reforms and destruction of the temple in Arad.

1. **Josiah became king and did what was right in the eyes of the Lord.**

   2 Kings 22:1-2: *Josiah was eight years old when he began to reign, and he reigned thirty-one years in Jerusalem. His mother's name was Jedidah the daughter of Adaiah of Bozkath. 2* ***And he did what was right in the eyes of the Lord*** *and walked in all the way of David his father, and he did not turn aside to the right or to the left.*

2. **Josiah's grandfather, Manasseh, was very wicked until God humbled him, and he repented. His father, Amon, was so wicked that his servants killed him (2 Kings 21).**

   Josiah's heritage was wicked and could have given him an excuse to live the same way. However, even at an extremely young age of 8, he loved the Lord and did what was right. Interestingly, the Book of the Law wasn't found until Josiah was 26 years old (2 Kings 22:3). This meant Josiah did what was right from a young age, even without Scripture to guide him.

3. **The Book of the Law (Bible) was found and read to Josiah.**

   2 Kings 22:8-11: *And Hilkiah the high priest said to Shaphan the secretary, "I have found the **Book of the Law** in the house of the Lord." And Hilkiah gave the book to Shaphan, and he read it. 9 And Shaphan the secretary came to the king, and reported to the king, "Your servants have*

Altar at the Israelite temple at Tel Arad

*emptied out the money that was found in the house and have delivered it into the hand of the workmen who have the oversight of the house of the Lord." 10 Then Shaphan the secretary told the king, "Hilkiah the priest has given me a book." And Shaphan read it before the king. 11 When the king heard the words of the **Book of the Law**, he tore his clothes.*

4. **Josiah read the Bible to his whole kingdom and made a covenant with them to follow the Lord.**

   2 Kings 23:1–3: *Then the king sent, and all the elders of Judah and Jerusalem were gathered to him. 2 And the king went up to the house of the Lord, and with him all the men of Judah and all the inhabitants of Jerusalem and the priests and the prophets, all the people, both small and great. And he read in their hearing all the words of the* **Book of the Covenant** *that had been found in the house of the Lord. 3 And the king stood by the pillar and made a covenant before the Lord, to walk after the Lord and to keep his commandments and his testimonies and his statutes with all his heart and all his soul, to perform the words of this covenant that were written in this book. And* **all the people joined in the covenant**.

5. **Josiah cleansed the temple and ordered that all the altars and shrines to the false gods be destroyed throughout the land (2 Kings 23:4–20). It was most likely Josiah who ordered the temple removed at Tel Arad.**

6. **Josiah reinstitutes and celebrates the Passover.**

   2 Chronicles 35:18: *No Passover like it had been kept in Israel since the days of Samuel the prophet. None of the kings of Israel had kept such a Passover as was kept by Josiah, and the priests and the Levites, and all Judah and Israel who were present, and the inhabitants of Jerusalem.*

Israelite temple at Arad

   2 Chronicles 35:7: *Then* **Josiah contributed** *to the lay people, as Passover offerings for all who were present, lambs and young goats from the flock to the number of 30,000, and 3,000 bulls; these were* **from the king's possessions**.

7. **There was no king like Josiah, who turned to the Lord with all his heart.**

    2 Kings 23:25: *Before him there was no king like him, who turned to the Lord with all his heart and with all his soul and with all his might, according to all the Law of Moses, nor did any like him arise after him.*

8. **Unfortunately, Josiah's two sons who reigned after him did not follow the Lord but acted wickedly (2 Kings 23:31–37).**

Faith Lesson from Arad

1. The Israelites in Arad set up their own temple and worshiped God their own way, which was forbidden to do. Do we realize that worshiping the right God in the wrong way is still wrong?

2. Josiah's heritage was rooted in sin, yet he chose to follow the Lord at a very young age. Do we realize that God can still use us mightily regardless of our past if we turn to Him with all our hearts as Josiah did?

Israelite Fortress at Tel Arad

3. Even though Josiah followed God with all his heart, his children chose evil. Each person has a free will to do as they please regardless of the kind of parents they have.

Journal/Notes:

Negev & Southern Israel Sites

Tel Beersheba

Location

1. Beersheba is located in the Negev, which is a semi-desert.
2. The tel of Beersheba lies a little east of the modern city, which is the region's largest city and administrative capital.
3. It's about 45 miles (70 km.) south of Jerusalem and about 30 miles (45 km.) from the Mediterranean Ocean.
4. It's located between the Beersheba and Hebron Streams (which are dry much of the time).
5. It was located on a significant travel route linking Africa and Egypt with Asia and Europe. The Nabateans, who were centralized in Petra, passed through here on caravans with trade goods.

Historical Background

1. Beersheba is the beginning place of God's master plan for the Nation of Israel.
2. In essence, each person has the same tendencies as the Nation of Israel. Therefore, when God wanted to speak to all mankind, He used Israel as the example (1 Cor. 10:11).
3. The name Negev means "dry land" in Hebrew, but the Bible often uses the term to refer to the southern part of Israel.
4. Because Beersheba is in the Negev, which receives an annual rainfall of 6–8 inches (18 cm.), there was not much population in the area, and most of the people living here were nomadic shepherds.
5. Beersheba was in the territory of the Philistines (Gen. 21:33–34).
6. After a conflict over Abraham's well, which he had dug in Beersheba, a covenant was made between Abimelech and

Abraham to settle the dispute (Gen. 21:25–34). To ratify the covenant, Abraham gave Abimelech seven ewe lambs. Therefore, Beersheba means "well of the oath" or "well of the seven lambs."

7. When the writers of Scripture wanted to speak of all Israel, they would often use the expression "from Dan (the northern-most city) to Beersheba" (the southern-most city).

Tel Beersheba

Places of Interest

1. Four-Horned Altar

   This altar belonged to cult worship or was misused by the Israelites as it doesn't comply with Scripture. Altars were to be made of "stones on which you have not used an iron tool" (Deut. 27:5). This altar used hand-shaped stones. The altar was likely one of those torn down during the religious reforms of King Josiah (2 Kings 23:8).

2. Abraham's Well – 230 ft. deep (70 m.)
3. Outer Gate
4. Inner Gate
5. City Square
6. Governor's Palace
7. Roman Bath Pools
8. Basement House
9. Four-room House
10. Casement Wall
11. Roman Fortress
12. Observation Tower
13. Storerooms

Negev & Southern Israel Sites

14. Street with Shops
15. Beersheba Stream
16. Hebron Stream
17. Water Cistern

Beersheba in the Bible

1. **About 2,000 years before Christ, God called Abraham from Mesopotamia to leave his family and possessions and journey to a new land with the promise that his descendants would become a great nation.**

   Genesis 12:1–3: *Now the Lord said to Abram, "Go from your country and your kindred and your father's house to the land that I will show you. 2 And I will make of you **a great nation**, and I will bless you and make your name great, so that you will be a blessing. 3 I will bless those who bless you, and him who dishonors you I will curse, and in you all the families of the earth shall be blessed."*

2. **After Abraham passed through the Land of Israel, he settled in the Negev area (Gen. 12:9).**

3. **When a severe famine came upon the land, Abraham left the Negev for a bit and went to Egypt (Gen. 12:10).**

4. **After the famine, Abraham returned to the Negev (close to Hebron), and God confirmed His covenant with him.**

   Genesis 13:14–17: *The Lord said to Abram, after Lot had separated from him, "Lift up your eyes and look from the place where you are, northward and southward and eastward and westward, 15 **for all the land that you see I will give to you and to your offspring forever. 16 I will make your offspring as the dust of the earth**, so that if one can count the dust of the earth, your offspring also can be counted. 17 Arise, walk through the length and the breadth of the land, for I will give it to you."*

   Abraham's Well

   The Abrahamic Covenant includes two promises: (1) a land, and (2) a nation of people. From this covenant comes the Nation of Israel and their land.

5. **After the destruction of Sodom and Gomorrah, Abraham settled in Beersheba and "Lived there many days" (Gen. 21:34), probably meaning the rest of his life.**

6. **Nearby to Beersheba, Hagar, the mother of Ismael, was sent away by Abraham. However, an angel of the Lord ministered to her, saying that her offspring would be blessed (Gen. 21:14–18).**

7. **Isaac, the son and heir Abraham and Sarah had waited all their lives to have, was born in Beersheba.**

8. **It was from Beersheba that Abraham journeyed with his son Isaac to Mount Moriah at Jerusalem, where God tested him to see if he would be willing to sacrifice his son Isaac as a burnt offering. Mount Moriah is the exact place that Solomon would later build the temple in Jerusalem where countless sacrifices would be made, the most significant being the sacrifice of Christ on the Cross.**

   Genesis 22:1–5: *After these things, God tested Abraham and said to him, "Abraham!" And he said, "Here am I." 2 He said, "Take your son,* *your only son Isaac, whom you love, and go to the land of **Moriah**, and offer him there as a burnt offering on one of the mountains of which I shall tell you." 3 So Abraham rose early in the morning, saddled his donkey, and took two of his young men with him, and his son Isaac. And he cut the wood for the burnt offering and arose and went to the place of which God had told him. 4 On the third day, Abraham lifted up his eyes and saw the place from afar. 5 Then*

Entering Tel Beersheba

Abraham said to his young men, "Stay here with the donkey; I and the boy will go over there and worship and come again to you."

Genesis 22:10–19: *Then Abraham reached out his hand and took the knife to slaughter his son. 11 But the angel of the LORD called to him from heaven and said, "Abraham, Abraham!" And he said, "Here am I." 12 He said, "Do not lay your hand on the boy or do anything to him, **for now I know that you fear God, seeing you have not withheld your son, your only son, from me**." 13 And Abraham lifted up his eyes and looked, and behold, behind him was a ram, caught in a thicket by his horns. And Abraham went and took the ram and offered it up as a burnt offering instead of his son. 14 So Abraham called the name of that place, "The LORD will provide"; as it is said to this day, "**On the mount of the LORD it shall be provided**." 15 And the angel of the LORD called to Abraham a second time from heaven 16 and said, "By myself I have sworn, declares the LORD, **because you have done this and have not withheld your son, your only son**, 17 I will surely bless you, and I will surely multiply your offspring as the stars of heaven and as the sand that is on the seashore. And your offspring shall possess the gate of his enemies, 18 and in your offspring shall all the nations of the earth be blessed, because you have obeyed my voice." 19 So Abraham returned to his young men, and they arose and went together to Beersheba. And Abraham lived at Beersheba.*

9. **It was at Beersheba that Isaac and Rebecca met, falling in love at first sight (Gen. 24:62–67).**

10. Isaac's son, Jacob, stole the birthright from his brother Esau while the family lived in Beersheba (Gen. 27).
11. Jacob lived in Beersheba when he and all his family moved to Egypt to live with Joseph (Gen. 46:45–47).

Four-Horned Altar

12. The Prophet Elijah came to Beersheba when he fled from Jezebel after the great showdown on Mount Carmel between God and the 450 prophets of Baal and the 400 prophets of Asherah. Elijah had the prophets killed, whom Jezebel supported, so he was running for his life.

Faith Lesson from Beersheba

1. Beersheba is the beginning place of God's sovereign master plan for the Nation of Israel, and through them, all mankind.
2. Beersheba played a key role in the lives of all the patriarchs.
3. Abraham left his family and country in Mesopotamia in obedience to God and settled in Beersheba.
4. God tested Abraham at Beersheba, and he proved he loved God more than any earthly treasure, even his own son.
5. Do we understand that God often tests us as well?
6. Do we understand that God's greatest question for us is, "What do you love more than me?"
7. Do I have anything in my life that stands between God and me?
8. Do I know what my "Isaac" is, and would I be willing to give it up to God if He asked me to?
9. Abraham is called "Our father of faith" because of his obedience and devotion to God. Do we have faith like Abraham?

Journal/Notes:

Negev & Southern Israel Sites

Bethlehem Overview

Location

1. Bethlehem is located 6 miles (9 km.) south of Jerusalem.
2. In Bible times, Bethlehem was a farming area with grainfields, and sheep and goats grazed the hillsides. Amazingly, little has changed over the past 3,000 years.
3. It's on the edge of the Judean Desert that lies to the southeast.
4. Bethlehem is in the West Bank but is very safe. Thousands visit its Christian sites each month with no issues.

Historical Background

1. Bethlehem was a Canaanite village before the conquest of the Israelites in around 1406 BC.
2. It means "House of Bread." Maybe this is so because many wheat and barley fields were in this area.

Places of Interest

1. Rachel's Tomb
2. Church of the Nativity
3. Shepherds' Fields
4. Herodian Fortress
5. Grainfields
6. Hillsides for livestock to graze on.
7. Deep Ravine – Maybe the valley David had in mind when he wrote Psalm 23.

Bethlehem in the Bible

1. **Jacob's wife, Rachel, died and was buried in Bethlehem.**

   Genesis 35:16–20: *Then they journeyed from Bethel. When they were still some distance from Ephrath [Bethlehem], Rachel went into labor, and she had hard labor. 17 And when her labor was at its hardest, the midwife said to her, "Do not fear, for you have another son." 18 And as her soul was departing (for she was dying), she called his name Ben-oni; but his father called him Benjamin. 19 So Rachel died, and she was buried on the way to Ephrath (that is, Bethlehem), 20 and Jacob set up a pillar over her tomb. It is the pillar of Rachel's tomb, which is there to this day.*

2. **Naomi was from Bethlehem, but because of a famine in Israel, her husband and two sons moved to Moab.**

   Ruth 1:1–2: *In the days when the judges ruled there was a famine in the land, and a man of **Bethlehem** in Judah went to sojourn in the country of Moab, he and his wife and his two sons. 2 The name of the man was Elimelech and the name of his wife, Naomi, and the names of his two sons were Mahlon and Chilion.*

3. **Naomi and Ruth returned from Moab to Bethlehem.**

   Ruth 1:22: *So Naomi returned, and Ruth the Moabite her daughter-*

in-law with her, who returned from the country of Moab. And they came to **Bethlehem** *at the beginning of barley harvest.*

4. **Ruth gleaned in the grainfields of Boaz in Bethlehem and then married Boaz (Boaz was the Great Grandfather of King David).**

   Ruth 2:1–2: *Now Naomi had a relative of her husband's, a worthy man of the clan of Elimelech, whose name was Boaz. 2 And Ruth the Moabite said to Naomi, "Let me go to the field and glean among the ears of grain after him in whose sight I shall find favor." And she said to her, "Go, my daughter."*

   Ruth 4:13–17: *So Boaz took Ruth, and she became his wife. And he went in to her, and the Lord gave her conception, and she bore a son. 14 Then the women said to Naomi, "Blessed be the Lord, who has not left you this day without a redeemer, and may his name be renowned in Israel! 15 He shall be to you a restorer of life and a nourisher of your old age, for your daughter-in-law who loves you, who is more to you*

   Shepherds' Field

   than seven sons, has given birth to him." 16 Then Naomi took the child and laid him on her lap and became his nurse. 17 And the women of the neighborhood gave him a name, saying, "A son has been born to Naomi." They named him Obed. He was the father of Jesse, the father of David.

5. **King David was from Bethlehem, so it is also called the "City of David."**

   1 Samuel 17:12: *Now David was the son of an Ephrathite of Bethlehem in Judah, named Jesse, who had eight sons. In the days of Saul, the man was already old and advanced in years.*

6. **David grew up in Bethlehem as a shepherd. Being a shepherd was a lonely, boring job that no one wanted. However, David put his time to good use and learned to play the harp, throw a sling, and grew to love the Lord. Many of the Psalms David wrote have their roots in the area around Bethlehem.**

7. **David was anointed king in Bethlehem.**

1 Samuel 16:1: *The Lord said to Samuel, "How long will you grieve over Saul, since I have rejected him from being king over Israel? Fill your horn with oil, and go. I will send you to Jesse the Bethlehemite, for I have provided for myself a king among his sons."*

1 Samuel 16:4: *Samuel did what the Lord commanded and came to* **Bethlehem**.

1 Samuel 16:6–7: *When they came, he looked on Eliab and thought, "Surely the Lord's anointed is before him." 7 But the Lord said to Samuel, "Do not look on his appearance or on the height of his stature, because I have rejected him. For the Lord sees not as man sees:* **man looks on the outward appearance, but the Lord looks on the heart**.*"*

Herodian Fortress

1 Samuel 16:11–13: *Then Samuel said to Jesse, "Are all your sons here?" And he said, "There remains yet the youngest, but behold, he is keeping the sheep." And Samuel said to Jesse, "Send and get him, for we will not sit down till he comes here." 12 And he sent and brought him in. Now he was ruddy and had beautiful eyes and was handsome. And the Lord said, "Arise, anoint him, for this is he." 13 Then Samuel took the horn of oil and anointed him in the midst of his brothers. And the Spirit of the Lord rushed upon David from that day forward.*

8. **King Herod the Great built a huge fortress called the "Herodian" that was located just outside of Bethlehem. It was built for his protection and glory.**

9. **Bethlehem was the prophesied birthplace of Christ.**

    Micah 5:2: *But you, O Bethlehem Ephrathah, who are too little to be among the clans of Judah, from you shall come forth for me one who is to be ruler in Israel, whose coming forth is from of old, from ancient days.*

    Luke 2:7: *And she gave birth to her firstborn son and wrapped him in swaddling clothes and laid him in a manger, because there was no place for them in the inn.*

10. Angels appeared to shepherds watching their flocks by night in Bethlehem.

Luke 2:8–16: *And there were shepherds living out in the fields nearby, keeping watch over their flocks at night. 9 And an angel of the Lord appeared to them, and the glory of the Lord shone around them, and they were filled with fear. 10 And the angel said to them, "Fear not, for behold, I bring you good news of great joy that will be for all the people. 11 For unto you is born this day in the **city of David**, a Savior, who is Christ the Lord. 12 And this will be a sign for you: you will find a baby wrapped in swaddling clothes and lying in a manger." 13 And suddenly there was with the angel a multitude of the heavenly host praising God*

*and saying, 14 "Glory to God in the highest, and on earth peace among those with whom he is pleased!" 15 When the angels went away from them into heaven, the shepherds said to one another, "Let us go over to **Bethlehem** and see this thing that has happened, which the Lord has made known to us." 16 And they went with haste and found Mary and Joseph, and the baby lying in a manger.*

11. Wise men (Magi) from the east visited and worshiped Christ in Bethlehem.

Matthew 2:1: *Now after Jesus was born in **Bethlehem** of Judea in the days of Herod the king, behold, wise men from the east came to Jerusalem saying, "Where is he who has been born king of the Jews? For we saw his star when it rose and have come to worship him."*

12. King Herod had all the male children 2 years and younger murdered in his attempt to kill Christ.

Matthew 2:16–18: *Then Herod, when he saw that he had been tricked by the wise men, became furious, and he sent and killed all the male children in Bethlehem and in all that region who were two years old or under, according to the time that he had ascertained from the wise men. 17 Then was fulfilled what was spoken by the prophet Jeremiah: 18 "A voice was heard in Ramah, weeping and loud lamentation, Rachel weeping for her children; she refused to be comforted, because they are no more."*

Grainfields (center) deep ravine (right)

Faith Lesson from Bethlehem

1. Bethlehem means "House of Bread." Jesus also refers to Himself as the Bread of life.
2. In the same way our bodies need bread to live, so our spirit needs Christ for nourishment and life. Are we feeding daily on God's Word and walking moment by moment in dependence on Him?
3. We have many godly examples of people from Bethlehem who walked with God, i.e., Naomi, Ruth, Boaz, and David.
4. Today, they are in heaven rejoicing in God's presence. Are we following their example and living for our eternal home as well?
5. David used his spare time shepherding wisely and learned many skills that He would eventually use to serve God. Are we developing our abilities to be better servants of Christ?
6. The Lord sees not as man sees: man looks on the outward appearance, but the Lord looks on the heart (1 Sam. 16:7). What kind of heart does God see in us?

Journal/Notes:

Negev & Southern Israel Sites

Bethlehem: Church of the Nativity

Location

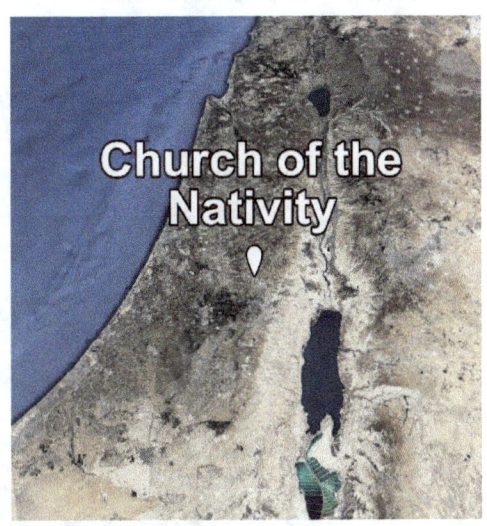

1. The Church of the Nativity is in Bethlehem, about 6 miles (9 km.) south of Jerusalem.
2. It's right beside Manger Square and Manger Street.
3. Bethlehem is in the West Bank but is very safe. Thousands of tourists visit its Christian sites each month with no issues whatsoever.

Historical Background

1. Shortly after Christ's ascension back to heaven, worshipers began marking the key places surrounding the life and events of Jesus.
2. Christ's birthplace was marked out, and worshipers began commemorating this site.
3. In 135 AD, Hadrian, a Roman governor, destroyed the Christian sites and built shrines to false gods on top of many of them. He also renamed Jerusalem to Aelia Capitolina and banned Jews from entering the city.
4. On top of Christ's birthplace, he erected a shrine to Adonis, the Greek god of beauty and desire.
5. Evidence that this was the birthplace of Jesus also surfaced in the writings of Justin Martyr in around 160 AD. It was also affirmed later by Origen and Eusebius in the 3rd century.
6. Helena, the mother of the Roman Emperor, Constantine, received Christ as her Savior and came to the Holy Land to build churches on key Christian sites.
7. Constantine and his mother, Helena, commissioned that the Church of the Nativity be built over the cave marking the birthplace of Jesus, and it was dedicated in 339 AD. It consisted of an octagonal floor plan and was placed directly over the cave. In the center of the octagonal part, a viewing area with a railing

provided a view of the cave. Part of the mosaic of the original floor has survived and can still be seen.

8. Jerome, who translated the Hebrew and Greek manuscripts into Latin (the language of the Roman Empire) to form what is called the Latin Vulgate, did much of his translation work in a cave beside the Church of the Nativity from 382–405 AD. He was later buried here, and today it's called Jerome's Grotto. His remains were carried to Rome by the Crusaders in around 1165.

9. The church was burned down during a Samaritan revolt in 529 AD.

10. Justinian, emperor of the Byzantine Empire, rebuilt a larger church in 565 AD that has survived to date. It is the oldest functioning church in the world.

11. The Church of the Nativity was the only church spared by the Persians during their conquest of the Holy Land in 614 AD because they saw paintings on the outside of the church honoring the Magi from the east who were fellow Persians.

12. The Crusaders renovated the church in around 1165 AD and painted murals on the pillars of the main nave.

13. The church has been neglected and renovated several times since the Crusader period to the present.

14. Today, the custody of the church is in the hands of the Roman Catholic, Armenian, and Greek Orthodox churches. The Greek Orthodox Church cares for the Grotto of the Nativity.

Church of the Nativity

Places of Interest

1. Entrance to the Church
   - Door of Humility – To provide a humble entrance and keep horsemen and carts from entering the church to loot it during

the Ottoman Period (1500 AD).
2. Entrance Lobby
3. Main Nave
    - Columns with Crusader murals.
    - Mosaics under the floor.
    - Fragments of 12th-century mosaics on the walls high above the columns.
4. High Altar (front part of the nave)
    - Mosaics of the original church on the left side of the High Altar.

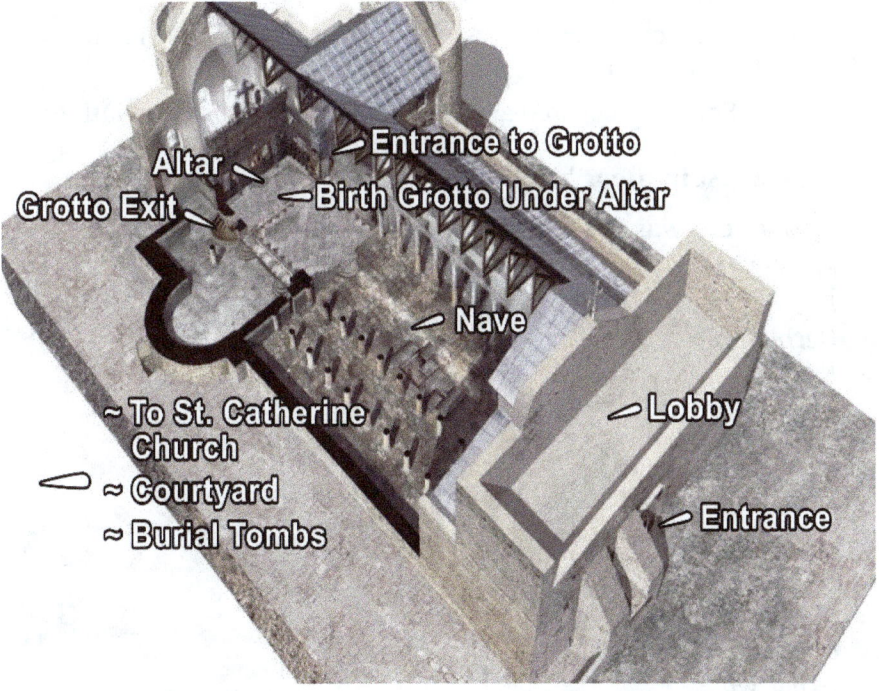

5. Birthplace Grotto
    - Located under the main altar.
    - The entrance is to the right of the altar, and the exit is to the left.
    - Manger where Christ was placed – on the right side of the grotto.
    - A 14-pointed star marking the birthplace of Christ is in the center of the grotto (14 points for the three sets of 14

generations in Matthew 1:17, and for the 14 Stations of the Via Dolorosa).
6. Church of St. Catherine
   - A Roman Catholic Church named after Catherine, a 4th-century martyr from Alexandria.
   - It was built upon the ruins of a 5th-century monastery and a 12th-century Crusader church.
   - Courtyard
   - Statue of Jerome in the courtyard.
   - Burial Caves – Jerome's Grotto
   - The burial caves are accessed by a narrow staircase inside the Church of St. Catherine on the right side.
7. Manger Square – Located across from the Church of the Nativity.

Birth of Christ in the Bible

1. **Bethlehem was the prophesied birthplace of Christ.**

   Micah 5:2: *But you, O **Bethlehem** Ephrathah, who are too little to be among the clans of Judah, from you shall come forth for me one who is to be ruler in Israel, whose coming forth is from of old, from ancient days.*

   Birthplace of Jesus marked by 14-point star

2. **Christ was born in Bethlehem as prophesied.**

   Luke 2:1–7: *In those days Caesar Augustus issued a decree that a census should be taken of the entire Roman world. 2 (This was the first census that took place while Quirinius was governor of Syria.) 3 And everyone went to his own town to register. 4 So Joseph also went up from the town of Nazareth in Galilee to Judea, to **Bethlehem** the town of David, because he belonged to the house and* line of David. 5 He went there to register with Mary, who was pledged to be married to him and was expecting a child. 6 While they were there, the time came for the baby to be born, 7 and she gave birth to her firstborn, a son. She wrapped him in cloths and placed him in a manger, because there was no room for them in the inn.

3. **Many angels appeared to the shepherds near Bethlehem who were watching their flocks.**

Luke 2:8–16: *And there were shepherds living out in the fields nearby, keeping watch over their flocks at night. 9 An angel of the Lord appeared to them, and the glory of the Lord shone around them, and they were terrified. 10 But the angel said to them, "Do not be afraid. I bring you good news of great joy that will be for all the people. 11 Today in the town of David a Savior has been born to you; he is Christ the Lord. 12 This will be a sign to you: You will find a baby*

Manger where Jesus was laid

wrapped in cloths and lying in a manger." 13 Suddenly a great company of the heavenly host appeared with the angel, praising God and saying, 14 "Glory to God in the highest, and on earth peace to men on whom his favor rests." 15 When the angels had left them and gone into heaven, the shepherds said to one another, "Let's go to **Bethlehem** *and see this thing that has happened, which the Lord has told us about." 16 So they hurried off and found Mary and Joseph, and the baby, who was lying in the manger.*

4. **Wise men (Magi) from the east visited and worshiped Christ in Bethlehem.**

Matthew 2:1–12: *Now after Jesus was born in Bethlehem of Judea in the days of Herod the king, behold, wise men from the east came to Jerusalem, 2 saying, "Where is he who has been born king of the*

Jews? For we saw his star when it rose and have come to worship him." 3 When Herod the king heard this, he was troubled, and all Jerusalem with him; 4 and assembling all the chief priests and scribes of the people, he inquired of them where the Christ was to be born. 5 They told him, "In Bethlehem of Judea, for so it is written by the prophet: 6 "'And you, O Bethlehem, in the land of Judah, are by no means least among the rulers of Judah; for from you shall come a ruler who will shepherd my people Israel.'" 7 Then Herod summoned the wise men secretly and ascertained from them what time the star had appeared. 8 And he sent them to Bethlehem, saying, "Go and search diligently for the child, and when you have found him, bring me word, that I too may come and worship him." 9 After listening to the king, they went on their way. And behold, the star that they had seen when it rose went before them until it came to rest over the place where the child was. 10 When they saw the star, they rejoiced exceedingly with great joy. 11 And going into the house they saw the child with Mary, his mother, and they fell down and worshiped him. Then, opening their treasures, they offered him gifts, gold and frankincense, and myrrh. 12 And being warned in a dream not to return to Herod, they departed to their own country by another way.

Nave of the church with mosaics under the floor

5. **Herod had all the male children 2 years and younger murdered in Bethlehem in his attempt to kill Christ.**

Matthew 2:16–18: *Then Herod, when he saw that he had been tricked by the wise men, became furious, and he sent and killed all the male children in **Bethlehem and in all that region** who were two years old or under, according to the time that he had ascertained from the wise men. 17 Then was fulfilled what was spoken by the prophet Jeremiah: 18 "A voice was heard in Ramah, weeping and loud lamentation, Rachel weeping for her children; she* *refused to be comforted, because they are no more."*

Faith Lesson from the Birth of Christ

1. Bethlehem was the prophesied birthplace of Christ.
2. Christ fulfilled over 300 prophecies regarding his first coming.
3. The birth of Christ was a historical supernatural event witnessed by many.
4. The fulfillment of prophecy proves Christ was the Son of God and that His Word is inspired.
5. Christ's birth, death, and resurrection were all miraculous events, also proving Christ to be the very Son of God.
6. Christ claimed to be God in the flesh and proved it by His supernatural life and miracles.
7. Do we believe Christ is the Son of God, and have we received Him as our Lord and Savior?

Courtyard with statue of Jerome

Journal/Notes:

Bethlehem: Herodian Fortress

Location

1. The Herodian (Herodium) was a fortress and palace of King Herod located about 3 miles (5 km.) south of Bethlehem.
2. It's on the edge of the Judean Wilderness.
3. It was built upon a natural mountain which gave it added protection.
4. It was massive in size and overshadowed everything in the area with its presence and majesty.

Historical Background

1. The Roman Empire appointed King Herod to rule Judea on behalf of Rome from 37 to 4 BC. He was the king in power when Christ was born.
2. He's most known as the one who killed all the babies in Bethlehem 2 years old and younger in his attempt to kill Jesus.

   Matthew 2:16: *Then Herod, when he saw that he had been tricked by the wise men, became furious, and he sent and **killed all the male children in Bethlehem** and in all that region who were two years old or under, according to the time that he had ascertained from the wise men.*
3. He was so powerful that with a mere spoken word, he could order a mass execution of children in Bethlehem without approval from anyone.
4. Everything in Israel was dominated by King Herod, and his Herodian Fortress was evidence of his domination and power.
5. He was also a master builder who was known for building things that defied nature and glorified his name.
   - He built Caesarea Maritime, which was a deep-water seaport

larger than any in Rome, Athens, or Greece.
- He built Masada that was a fortress of protection and a winter palace. It had supplies for 1,000 people for 10 years.
- He enlarged the Temple Mount, which was an engineering masterpiece.
- He built a new temple for the Jews that was unparalleled in glory, size, and beauty.
- He built a massive building over the Caves of the Patriarchs in Hebron.
- He built this Herodian Fortress, named after himself, among other accomplishments.

6. War was common in his day, so the Herodian was built to protect himself and his kingship from those who tried to kill or remove him. The Herodian was on the highest mountain in the Judean Desert.
7. He had a great fear of betrayal from others attempting to usurp his throne. He had two of his sons strangled, killed numerous in-laws, and ordered his oldest son to be beheaded just before he died. He even had one of his wives murdered out of fear that she was in a plot to betray him.
8. Construction of the Herodian began in 25 BC using thousands of slaves. Herod reshaped the summit of the hill to create a pleasure palace and fortress that was virtually impregnable.

The Herodian

9. The Herodian was the 3rd largest palace in the known world at the time of Herod, and it was a monument to his power and glory.
10. It could be seen from many miles away and rose in dominance and prestige.
11. It covered 45 acres (18 hectares) and had a small luxurious city at

its base that included swimming pools, spas, a theater, and all the luxuries life could afford. An aqueduct brought water from a spring nearly 4 miles (6 km.) away.
12. On top of the Herodian were four towers that gave it a commanding view of the Judean Desert, the Dead Sea, and the mountains of Moab. By using mirrors to reflect the sun, Herod could send messages from the Herodian to Jerusalem, Masada, and other places.
13. Herod is remembered as a jealous self-serving person who built his own kingdom for his own glory. Because he was so despised and hated, at his death he ordered many prominent Jews to be killed so there would be weeping in Israel. He died at the age of 69 and was buried at the Herodian.
14. Today, all that's left of Herod's kingdom and glory are ancient ruins.
15. The Herodian has been used for defense and religious purposes after the time of Herod to the present.

Places of Interest
1. Lower Section
   - Park Entrance
   - Ballista balls at the park entrance.
   - Water Pool
   - City Ruins
   - Colonnade Pillars
   - Roman Garden
   - Staircase going up the mountain.
2. Upper Section
   - Herodian Palace and Fortress
   - Four Towers of the Palace (north, east, west, and south)
   - Synagogue (used from 66–70 AD)
   - Mikvah
   - Bathhouse
   - Cisterns
   - Bar Kokhba Revolt Tunnels (132–136 AD)
   - Tunnels

Negev & Southern Israel Sites

- Theater
- Herod's Tomb

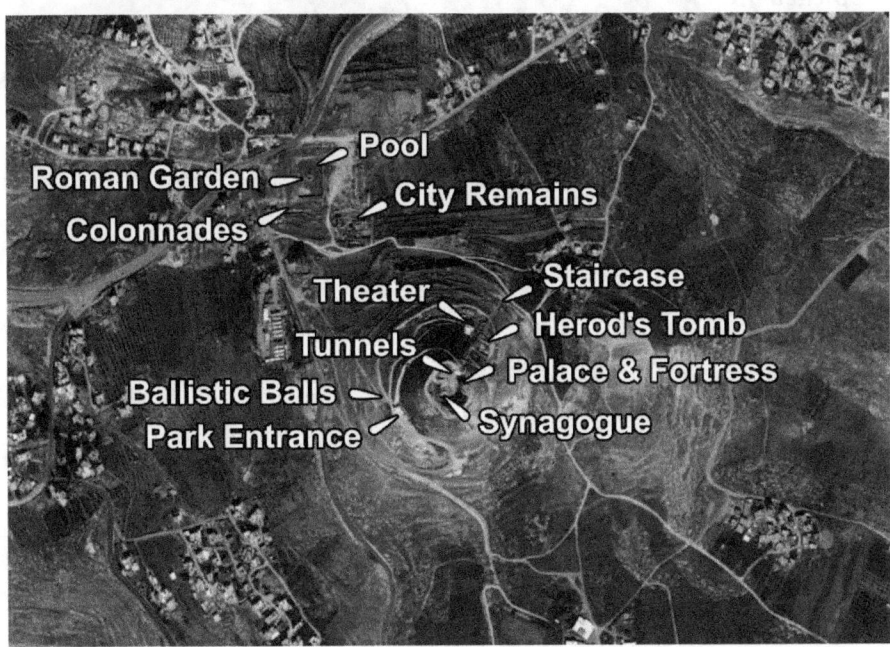

A Contrast of Two Kingdoms in the Bible

1. **Christ is the eternal majestic King of His kingdom.**

   Isaiah 9:6–7: *For to us a **child is born**, to us a son is given; and the government shall be upon his shoulder, and his name shall be called **Wonderful Counselor, Mighty God, Everlasting Father, Prince of Peace**. 7 Of the increase of his government and of peace there will be no end, on the throne of David and over his kingdom, to establish it and to uphold it with justice and with righteousness **from this time forth and forevermore**. The zeal of the Lord of hosts will do this.*

   Micah 5:2: *But you, O Bethlehem Ephrathah, who are too little to be among the clans of Judah, from you shall come forth for me one who is to be ruler in Israel, whose coming forth is from of old, from **ancient days**.*

   John 8:58–59: *Jesus said to them, "Truly, truly, I say to you, before Abraham was, **I AM**." 59 So they picked up stones to throw at him, but Jesus hid himself and went out of the temple.*

   John 10:31–33: *The Jews picked up stones again to stone him. 32 Jesus answered them, "I have shown you many good works from the Father; for which of them are you going to stone me?" 33 The Jews answered him, "It is not for a good work that we are going to stone you but for blasphemy, because you, being a man, **make yourself God**."*

   Pool & Roman Garden at the base of the Herodian

   Revelation 22:12–13: *Behold, I am coming soon, bringing my recompense with me, to repay each one for what he has done. 13 I am the **Alpha and the Omega**, the first and the last, the beginning and the end.*

2. **Unlike Herod, who only cared about building his own kingdom, Christ came as a lowly servant to serve others.**
   - Christ was born in a humble manger in the small frontier town

of Bethlehem.
- He owned no home and had nowhere to lay His head.
- He held no public office.
- He rode into Jerusalem on the colt of a donkey, which was a lowly symbol of peace.
- He washed His disciples' feet.
- He died a criminal's death between two thieves.

3. **Unlike Herod, who glorified himself, Christ set aside His glory to become an obedient servant, even unto death on a cross.**

   Philippians 2:5–11: *Have this attitude in yourselves which was also in Christ Jesus, 6 who, although He existed in the form of God, did not regard* **equality with God a thing to be grasped**, *7 but emptied Himself, taking the form of a bond-servant, and being made in the likeness of men. 8 Being found in appearance as a man,* **He humbled Himself** *by becoming obedient to the point of death, even death on a cross. 9 For this reason also, God highly exalted Him, and bestowed on Him the name which is above every name, 10 so that at the name of Jesus every knee will bow, of those who are in heaven and on earth and under the earth, 11 and that every tongue will confess that Jesus Christ is Lord, to the glory of God the Father.*

Herodian Palace on top of the Herodian

4. **Unlike Herod, whose kingdom came to ruins, Christ changed people and the course of history like no other person.**

Faith Lesson from the Herodian Fortress

1. Herod mainly cared about his own glory and kingdom. What about us? Are we more like King Herod or King Jesus?
2. We all have an element of King Herod living within us. Are we

going to follow those tendencies and desires?

1 John 2:15–17: *Do not love the world or the things in the world. If anyone loves the world, the love of the Father is not in him. 16 For all that is in the world—**the desires of the flesh, and the desires of the eyes, and pride of life**—is not from the Father but is from the world. 17 And the world is passing away along with its desires, but whoever does the will of God abides forever.*

View of the pool and city ruins from the top of the Herodian

3. Do we have a prideful attitude like Herod or a humble spirit like Christ?
4. Are we mainly building our own kingdom or God's?
5. What will be our legacy, and what will we leave behind?

   Matthew 6:19–21: *Do not lay up for yourselves treasures on earth, where moth and rust destroy and where thieves break in and steal, 20 but lay up for yourselves treasures in heaven, where neither moth nor rust destroys and where thieves do not break in and steal. 21 **For where your treasure is, there your heart will be also**.*

Journal/Notes:

Bethlehem: Shepherds' Field

Location

1. There are two main sites that have their own Shepherds' Field, where the angels appeared to the shepherds announcing Christ's birth. Less than a half-mile (1 km.) separates them from one another.

    - Franciscan Shepherds' Field (the most visited as it's more easily accessed and is set up for tourists).
    - The Greek Orthodox Shepherds' Field.
2. Both sites have substantial archaeological evidence and tradition supporting them. However, the Greek Orthodox site has more ruins and longer continuous usage.
3. Both places are located about a mile (2 km.) east of Bethlehem in the Beit Sahour village. The Church of the Nativity can be seen from each site.
4. Because the sites are so close to one another, it's very possible that the angels' appearance was seen from both places as there could have easily been numerous shepherds in close proximity. There are also various other ruins, churches, and monasteries in the area, which testify to the fact that this event happened here.

Historical Background

General Evidence

1. At the end of the 4th century, Jerome, who was translating the Hebrew and Greek Bible manuscripts into Latin at the Church of the Nativity, mentioned that the church in Jerusalem celebrated a feast-day at the Church of the Shepherds in this area on Christmas Eve.
2. In 384 AD, the pilgrim Egeria was shown the church called "At the

Shepherds" in a valley near Bethlehem. She reported, *"A big garden is there now, protected by a neat wall all around, and also there is a very splendid cave with an altar."*

3. In the 7th century, Bishop Archulph spoke of a burial place of three shepherds in the church at the Shepherds' Field.
4. In the 12th century, Peter the Deacon, a Benedictine monk, quoted an anonymous pilgrim who said, *"Not far from there, there is a church called of the Shepherds, where a large garden is fully enclosed by a wall, and there, there is a very luminous grotto which has an altar where an angel, appearing to the shepherds in a vigil, announced the birth of Christ."*

Franciscan Shepherds' Field

1. It has a cave with a soot-blackened roof that has been partly enclosed to make a modern chapel.
2. A church built in the 4th century was erected by the cave.
3. The church was destroyed by the time the Crusaders arrived, but pilgrims continued to visit and commemorate this site.

Franciscan Shepherds' Church

4. It has ruins of a monastery dating from the 4th century to the 7th century.
5. A large complex of caves containing Mikvahs, tunnels, and rooms can be found here.
6. Today, above the cave is a modern church shaped like a tent and decorated with a bronze angel that was built near the ruins of an ancient monastery in 1953.

Greek Orthodox Shepherds' Field

1. The original church was in a cave located on the site.
2. Helena, the mother of Constantine, modified the cave into a church in 326 AD. It is the only original church Helena built that has survived to this day.

Negev & Southern Israel Sites

3. In the 5th century, a barrel-vaulted roof was built on the cave-church, and a monastery was built on the site later.
4. Above the 5th-century cave-church, a Byzantine chapel was built that was replaced by a larger church, which was destroyed in 614 AD. The Byzantine church and monastery were rebuilt in the 7th century and survived until the 10th century.
5. In 1972, in order to build a new church above the cave-church, excavations verified the remains of three different churches dating to the 5th, 6th, and 7th centuries.

Greek Orthodox Shepherds' Church

6. The cave-church Helena built served the Orthodox community from the 4th century to 1955.
7. Today, a new large church has been built, the 4th-century cave-church has been restored, and the remains of the upper church and monastery have been preserved.
8. According to tradition dating from the 4th century, this site was associated with the place where Jacob pastured his flock and built Mignal Eder (Tower of the Flocks), referred to in Genesis 35:16. The remains of the base of this tower are still visible today.
9. If Mignal Eder is the site where Jacob erected a tower in Rachel's memory, this would also be the biblical location of Rachel's Tomb, and Jacob would have lived in this area for some time.

Places of Interest

1. Rachel's Tomb.
2. Church of the Nativity
3. Franciscan Shepherds' Field
4. Greek Orthodox Shepherds' Field
    - Mignal Eder Tower

5. Fields of Boaz

Shepherds' Fields in the Bible

1. **The Greek Orthodox Church site is associated with Mignal Eder, the place Jacob erected a tower of memorial to Rachel after her death.**

    Genesis 35:16–21: *Then they journeyed from Bethel. When they were still some distance from Ephrath [Bethlehem], Rachel went into labor, and she had hard labor. 17 And when her labor was at its hardest, the midwife said to her, "Do not fear, for you have another son." 18 And as her soul was departing (for she was dying), she called his name Ben-oni; but his father called him Benjamin. 19 So Rachel died, and she was buried on the way to Ephrath (that is, Bethlehem), 20 and Jacob set up a pillar over her tomb. It is the pillar of Rachel's tomb, which is there to this day. 21 Israel journeyed on and pitched his tent beyond the tower of Eder.*

2. **Ruth gleaned in the grainfields of Boaz and then married him (Boaz was the Great Grandfather of King David).**

    Ruth 2:1–2: *Now Naomi had a relative of her husband's, a worthy man of the clan of Elimelech, whose name was Boaz. 2 And Ruth the Moabite said to Naomi, "Let me go to the field and glean among the ears of grain after him in whose sight I shall find favor." And she said* to her, "Go, my daughter."

3. **Angels appeared to the shepherds out in the field, watching their flocks by night.**

   Luke 2:8–14: *And in the same region there were shepherds out in the field, keeping watch over their flock by night. 9 And an angel of the Lord appeared to them, and the glory of the Lord shone around them, and they were filled with great fear. 10 And the angel said to them, "Fear not, for behold, I bring you good news of great joy that will be for all the people. 11 For unto you is born this day in the city of David a Savior, who is Christ the Lord. 12 And this will be a sign for you: you will find a baby wrapped in swaddling cloths and lying in a manger." 13 And suddenly there was with the angel a multitude of the heavenly host praising God and saying, 14 "Glory to God in the highest, and on earth peace among those with whom he is pleased!"*

   Fields by Bethlehem

4. **The shepherds went in haste to see Jesus.**

   Luke 2:15–16: *When the angels went away from them into heaven, the shepherds said to one another, "Let us go over to Bethlehem and see this thing that has happened, which the Lord has made known to us." 16 And they went with haste and found Mary and Joseph, and the baby lying in a manger.*

5. **The shepherds spread the good news of Jesus' birth and returned, glorifying and praising God.**

   Luke 2:17–20: *And when they saw it, they made known the saying that had been told them concerning this child. 18 And all who heard it wondered at what the shepherds told them. 19 But Mary treasured up all these things, pondering them in her heart. 20 And the shepherds returned, glorifying and praising God for all they had heard and seen, as it had been told them.*

Faith Lesson from the Shepherds' Fields

1. The shepherds were the first to hear the announcement of Jesus' birth.
2. Shepherds were considered among the lowliest people. To be a shepherd was to be a nobody. It was a boring, lonely, despised job no one wanted.
3. Because Christ came to save all people and show his humility, the angels appeared to the shepherds as a sign that the "Good News" was available for all, from the lowliest shepherds to the noblest kings (the Magi).

Ruins of Mignal Eder Tower

4. Do we believe salvation is for everyone?
5. Are we humble like the shepherds were?
6. The shepherds went in haste to see Jesus. Do we show zeal and fervor in our desire to be with Jesus?
7. The shepherds spread the good news about Jesus. Do we share the good news (gospel) with others as well?

Journal/Notes:

Negev & Southern Israel Sites

Beth-Shemesh

Location

1. Beth-Shemesh lies 13 miles (21 km.) west of Jerusalem and 20 miles (32 km.) east of the Mediterranean Sea. It's on Hwy. 38, about 5.5 miles (8 km.) south of Hwy. 1.

2. Beth-Shemesh was the most important city in the Sorek Valley as it was a guard-city to both east-west and north-south traffic through the region.
3. It was a border city between Judah and Dan that was given to the Levites.
4. Just across the valley (north) is the town of Zorah, where Samson lived. Some ruins and his tomb can be seen today.
5. Down the Sorek Valley (west) a short distance was the town of Timnah, the hometown of Samson's first wife, and the area where his girlfriend Delilah lived.
6. Beth-Shemesh means "House of the Sun" and probably got its name from sun worship by the Canaanites.
7. Beth-Shemesh is most known as the place where the Ark of the Covenant arrived when the Philistines returned it as found in 1 Samuel 6.

Historical Background

1. Beth-Shemesh was a large thriving city belonging to the Canaanites when the Israelites arrived in about 1406 BC.
2. The Philistines were part of the Canaanite people group who lived in the land (Gen. 21:34). They possessed iron and were the high-tech people of the day.
3. At the time of Judges and 1 Samuel (1050 AD), the Philistines had a stronghold in the coastal plain area.

Negev & Southern Israel Biblical Sites Guide

4. As the Philistines gained territory, they moved inland. Beth-Shemesh and the cities in the Sorek Valley were affected and became border towns between the Philistines and the Israelites.
5. Samson, who lived across from Beth-Shemesh in Zorah, engaged in battle with the Philistines to liberate the area from their grasp and return it to the Israelites.
6. The Philistines worshiped the false god, Dagon, who was supposedly the father of Baalsabul, or Baal. He was a fish god of fertility and was represented as a half-man, half-fish creature.

Places of Interest

1. Tel Beth-Shemesh
   - 5th-Century AD Byzantine Monastery
   - Underground Water Reservoir
   - Northern Double Chambered Gate
   - Southern Gate
   - Mosque Ruins
   - Tombs

- Large rock where the Israelites likely sacrificed the oxen who pulled the cart after receiving the Ark of the Covenant from the Philistines.
2. Sorek Valley
3. Nahal Sorek Stream
4. Zorah
    - Samson's Tomb
5. Tel Timnah
6. Modern Beth-Shemesh

Beth-Shemesh in the Bible

1. **God gave the Israelites over to the Philistines because they had done evil in His sight.**

    Judges 13:1: *And the people of Israel again did what was evil in the sight of the LORD, so the LORD gave them into the hand of the Philistines for forty years.*

2. **God raised up Samson to begin the deliverance of the area from the hand of the Philistines (Judg. 13–16).**

3. **Not long after the death of Samson, the Ark of the Covenant was captured in a battle against the Philistines. This was due**

to judgment against the priest Eli and his two sons, Hophni and Phinehas, who all died in battle because of their wickedness (1 Sam. 4).

4. **The Philistines believed they were victorious in battle because their god, Dagon, was stronger than the true God of the Israelites. As a result, the Philistines took the Ark to the temple of their god, Dagon, to honor him for the victory.**

5. **However, God made the false god, Dagon, fall down in worship before the Ark.**

   1 Samuel 5:1–4: *When the Philistines captured the ark of God, they brought it from Ebenezer to Ashdod. 2 Then the Philistines took the ark of God and brought it into the house of Dagon and set it up beside Dagon. 3 And when the people of Ashdod rose early the next day, behold, Dagon had fallen face downward on the ground before the ark of the LORD. So they took Dagon and put him back in his place. 4 But when they rose early on the next morning, behold, Dagon had fallen face downward on the ground before the ark of the LORD, and the head of Dagon and both his hands were lying cut off on the threshold. Only the trunk of Dagon was left to him.*

   Tel Beth-Shemesh

6. **God sent the Philistines many sicknesses as a result of possessing the Ark. So they moved it from town to town, thinking their diseases were just coincidental.**

7. **Finally, they realized that it was God who was behind their diseases and decided to send the Ark of the Covenant back to the Israelites.**

8. **The Philistines prepare to return the Ark to the Israelites in Beth-Shemesh.**

   1 Samuel 6:1–9: *The ark of the LORD was in the country of the Philistines seven months. 2 And the Philistines called for the priests and the diviners and said, "What shall we do with the ark of the*

LORD? Tell us with what we shall send it to its place." 3 They said, "If you send away the ark of the God of Israel, do not send it empty, but by all means return him a guilt offering. Then you will be healed, and it will be known to you why his hand does not turn away from you." 4 And they said, "What is the guilt offering that we shall return to him?" They answered, "Five golden tumors and five golden mice, according to the number of the lords of the Philistines, for the same plague was on all of you and on your lords. 5 So you must make images of your tumors and images of your mice that ravage the land, and give glory to the God of Israel. Perhaps he will lighten his hand from off you and your gods and your land. 6 Why should you harden your hearts as the Egyptians and Pharaoh hardened their hearts? After he had dealt severely with them, did they not send the people away, and they departed? 7 Now then, take and prepare a new cart and two milk cows on which there has never come a yoke, and yoke the cows to the cart, but take their calves home, away from them. 8 And take the ark of the LORD and place it on the cart and put in a box at its side the figures of gold, which you are returning to him as a guilt offering. Then send it off and let it go its way 9 and watch. If it goes up on the way to its own land, to **Beth-Shemesh**, then it is he who has done us this great harm, but if not, then we shall know that it is not his hand that struck us; it happened to us by coincidence."

Tel Beth-Shemesh & Sorek Valley

9. **The Ark miraculously arrives at Beth-Shemesh.**

1 Samuel 6:10–13: *The men did so and took two milk cows and yoked them to the cart and shut up their calves at home. 11 And they put the ark of the LORD on the cart and the box with the golden mice and the images of their tumors. 12 And the cows went straight in the direction of **Beth-Shemesh** along one highway, lowing as they went. They turned neither to the right nor to the left, and the lords of the*

Philistines went after them as far as the border of **Beth-Shemesh**. 13 Now the people of **Beth-Shemesh** were reaping their wheat harvest in the valley. And when they lifted up their eyes and saw the ark, they rejoiced to see it.

10. The Israelites offer a burnt offering to the Lord in gratitude for receiving the Ark.

1 Samuel 6:14–16: *The cart came into the field of Joshua of **Beth-Shemesh** and stopped there. A great stone was there. And they split up the wood of the cart and offered the cows as a burnt offering to the LORD. 15 And the Levites took down the ark of the LORD and the box that was beside it, in which were the golden figures, and set them upon the great stone. And the men of **Beth-Shemesh** offered burnt offerings and sacrificed sacrifices on that day to the LORD. 16 And when the five lords of the Philistines saw it, they returned that day to Ekron.*

11. The Beth-Shemesh area is where Philip the Evangelist witnessed to the Ethiopian Eunuch.

Acts 8:26–31: *Now an angel of the Lord said to Philip, "Rise and go toward the south to the **road that goes down from Jerusalem to Gaza**." This is a desert place. 27 And he rose and went. And there was an Ethiopian, a eunuch, a court official of Candace, queen of the Ethiopians, who was in charge of all her treasure. He had come to Jerusalem to worship 28 and was returning,*

Road from Jerusalem to Gaza in the Sorek Valley

seated in his chariot, and he was reading the prophet Isaiah. 29 And the Spirit said to Philip, "Go over and join this chariot." 30 So Philip ran to him and heard him reading Isaiah the prophet and asked, "Do you understand what you are reading?" 31 And he said, "How can I, unless someone guides me?" And he invited Philip to come up and sit with him.

Faith Lesson from Beth-Shemesh

1. The Israelites adopted the sinful culture of those around them and did evil in the sight of the Lord. Am I careful not to adopt the sinful lifestyles and beliefs of the culture in which I live?

2. Even though the Israelites sinned and failed to be a faithful witness to the surrounding nations, God protected His glory and showed Himself to them as the true and living God. Am I a faithful witness to my culture in living out God's truth and reflecting His glory?

Northern City Gate of Beth-Shemesh

3. Do I use the miracles God has done in my life as a tool to witness and teach others who God is?

4. Like Philip, am I obedient in listening to God's voice and sharing the gospel when He prompts me?

Journal/Notes:

En Gedi

Location

1. En Gedi is on the west side of the lower Dead Sea area about 11 miles (17 km.) north of Masada on Hwy. 90.
2. It's a beautiful oasis fed by a large spring in a barren, dry place.

Historical Background

1. The Canaanites inhabited en Gedi during the time of Abraham and Lot.
2. The Dead Sea basin was once like a Garden of the Lord.

    Genesis 13:10–12: *Lot lifted up his eyes and saw all the valley of the Jordan, that it was **well watered everywhere**—this was **before the Lord destroyed Sodom and Gomorrah**—**like the garden of the Lord**, like the land of Egypt as you go to Zoar. 11 So Lot chose for himself all the valley of the Jordan, and Lot journeyed eastward. Thus, they separated from each other. 12 Abram settled in the land of Canaan, while Lot settled in the cities of the valley, and moved his tents as far as **Sodom**.*

3. Due to the abundant water supply, the village by En Gedi Park has had a long history of habitation from ancient days to the present.
4. Today, this area is extremely dry, and En Gedi is an oasis of living water in the desert.

Places of Interest

1. Park Entrance
2. Hiking Trail
3. Nahal David Stream
4. Lower Pools
5. Upper Pools
6. Upper Waterfall

7. Synagogue at Tel Goren (Jorn)
8. Ancient and Modern En Gedi Town
9. Dead Sea

En Gedi in the Bible

1. **En Gedi was used in a love poem in the book of Song of Solomon.**

   Song of Solomon 1:14: *My beloved is to me a cluster of henna blossoms in the vineyards of **En Gedi**.*

2. **In the Millennial Reign of Christ on earth, God speaks of how He will change the Dead Sea region again to be like a garden due to a supernatural river flowing from Jerusalem.**

   Ezekiel 47:9–10: *And wherever the river goes, every living creature that swarms will live, and there will be very many fish. For this water goes there, that the waters of the sea may become fresh; so everything will live where the river goes. 10 Fishermen will stand beside the sea. **From En Gedi to Eneglaim** it will be a place for the spreading of nets. Its fish will be of very many kinds, like the fish of the Great Sea.*

3. **En Gedi was one of David's main hideouts when Saul was**

pursuing his life.

1 Samuel 23:28–29: *So Saul returned from pursuing after David and went against the Philistines. Therefore, that place was called the Rock of Escape. 29 And David went up from there and lived in the strongholds of **En Gedi**.*

4. **En Gedi is a perfect example of living water in the desert.**
   - The Israelites were a desert people whose whole history was related to the desert. Abraham, Isaac, Jacob, Joseph, along with the Israelite's time in Egypt, and their wandering in the desert for 40 years, all took place in a desert. Also, much of Israel is a desert as well.
   - The Israelites fully knew that living water meant life and survival.

5. **God used the desert and living water as examples of judgment upon Israel.**

   Jeremiah 2:12–13: *Be appalled, O heavens, at this; be shocked, be utterly desolate, declares the LORD, 13 for my people have committed two evils: they have forsaken me, **the fountain of living waters**, and **hewed out cisterns for themselves**, broken cisterns that can hold no water.*

   En Gedi ravine

6. **God used desert imagery to show how those who abandon Him are like a parched desert without water.**

   Jeremiah 17:5–8: *Thus says the LORD: "**Cursed is the man who trusts in man** and makes flesh his strength, whose heart turns away from the LORD. 6 He is like a **shrub in the desert**, and shall not see any good come. He shall dwell in the **parched places of the wilderness**, in an uninhabited salt land. 7 **Blessed is the man who trusts in the LORD**, whose trust is the LORD. 8 He is like a tree planted by water, that sends out its roots by the stream, and does not fear when heat comes, for its leaves remain green, and is not anxious in the year of drought, for it does not cease to bear fruit."*

7. **Christ referred to Himself as the source of living water.**

   John 7:37–38: *On the last day of the feast, the great day, Jesus stood up and cried out, "If anyone thirsts, let him **come to me and drink**. 38 Whoever believes in me, as the Scripture has said, 'Out of his heart will **flow rivers of living water**."*

Faith Lesson from En Gedi

1. Living Water in the Bible refers to spiritual life and vitality found only in being right with God.
2. Stagnant water is full of sickness and diseases and refers to the person who lives life without being right with God.
3. Have we received Christ, the source of living water?
4. Do we fellowship regularly with God in order to receive living water for our souls?
5. Do we read God's Word, which gives living water to our spirits and nourishes our hearts?
6. Are we seeking to find life and joy in our own pursuits and neglecting our relationship with God?

   *Be appalled, O heavens, at this; be shocked, be utterly desolate, declares the LORD, 13 for my people have committed two evils: they have forsaken me, the **fountain of living waters**, and **hewed out cisterns for themselves**, broken cisterns that can hold no water* (Jer. 2:12–13).

Upper waterfall

Journal/Notes:

Exodus, Red Sea, and Mount Sinai

Location

1. For many years it was believed that the Israelites crossed the Suez finger of the Red Sea just southeast of what is now Cairo, Egypt. However, there are no deep bodies of water in these areas but just shallow marshes and lakes. For this reason, the biblical account of this astounding miracle has been attempted to be discredited or erased altogether by liberal scholars.

2. Many recent archeologists and scholars now believe the Israelites crossed the Red Sea at the Aqaba finger of the Red Sea and that Mount Sinai is in Midian, which is part of modern-day Saudi Arabia.

Historical Background

1. God called Abraham and promised him He would make a great nation out of his offspring. Abraham obeyed and left everything to follow God.
2. Abraham birthed Isaac, who birthed Jacob, who birthed 12 sons. God changed Jacob's name to Israel.
3. Jacob and his 12 sons moved to Egypt according to God's sovereign plan (about 70–75 total people).
4. The Israelites spent 430 years in Egypt (30 years as free people under Joseph and 400 years as slaves). During this time, they grew into a nation of around 2.5 to 3 million people.
5. God performed a miraculous deliverance of the Israelites from Egypt by performing 10 amazing miracles.
6. The last miracle, known as the Passover, happened when God killed the firstborn of all the Egyptians who did not put the blood

of a lamb over the doorposts of their homes.

Places of Interest

1. Egypt
2. Goshen
3. Suez Finger of the Red Sea
4. Traditional Red Sea Crossing Place
5. Sinai Peninsula
6. Aqaba Finger of Red Sea
7. Nuweiba Beach
8. Saudi Arabia Beach
9. Red Sea Crossing
10. Elim
11. Caves of Jethro
12. Rephidim
13. Mount Sinai

The Exodus, Red Sea Crossing, and Mount Sinai in the Bible

1. **How many Israelites left Egypt and crossed the Red Sea?**

   Exodus 12:37: *Now the sons of Israel journeyed from Rameses to Succoth, about* **six hundred thousand men** *on foot, aside from children.*

   Using the number of 600,000 men only, we can estimate that there were probably 2.5 to 3 million Israelites.

2. **How many Egyptian soldiers were chasing the Israelites?**

   Exodus 14:6–7: *So he made his chariot ready and took his people with him; 7 and he took six hundred select chariots, and all the other chariots of Egypt with officers over all of them.*

   According to Josephus, a historian writer, there were 50,000 horsemen and 200,000 footmen, all armed.

3. **Did the Israelites cross the Red Sea by Egypt?**

   For many years, it has been generally believed that the Israelites crossed the Suez finger of the Red Sea just east of Cairo, Egypt. However, the sea is not very deep there, so many have discredited the biblical miracle by claiming the Israelites crossed in shallow marshes of water.

   It should be noted that over the years, no archaeological evidence has supported this Red Sea crossing location. It also would have been virtually impossible for such a large army to drown in the shallow lakes and marshes in this area.

4. **Over the past several decades, substantial archeological investigation shows convincing evidence for a different location for the Red Sea crossing.**

   The new location places the crossing at Nuweiba Beach on the Aqaba finger of the Red Sea about 40 miles (64 km.) south of Eilat,

Israel.

5. **God said he brought the Israelites out of Egypt on the very same day they left.**

   Exodus 12:51: *And on that same day the Lord brought the sons of Israel **out of the land of Egypt** by their hosts.*

   The Red Sea crossing happened after they had left Egypt. The border of Egypt at that time was the Suez finger of the Red Sea. Any place the Israelites would have crossed the sea in this area they would still have been in Egypt and not outside of it.

6. **The Suez finger of the Red Sea is about 72 miles (116 km.) south of Goshen (place where the Israelites lived and departed Egypt). However, the land directly east of Goshen is dry and easily crossable.**

   The Israelites had exited Egypt on the same day they left. The route directly east of Goshen would have allowed them to leave Egypt on dry ground. Afterward, they would have been in the wilderness of Sinai, which fits well with the biblical narrative, as we will see in the next point.

7. **Scripture strongly indicates that the Israelites traveled a long time through a wilderness before crossing the Red Sea.**

   Exodus 13:18–22: *Hence, God led the people around by the **way of the wilderness to the Red Sea**; and the sons of Israel went up in martial array from the land of Egypt. 19 Moses took the bones of Joseph with him, for he had made the sons of Israel solemnly swear, saying, "God will surely take care of you, and you shall carry my bones from here with you." 20 Then they set out from Succoth and camped in Etham on the edge of the wilderness. 21 The Lord was going before them in a pillar of cloud by day to lead them on the way, and in a pillar of fire by night to give them light, that they* might **travel by day and by night**. *22 He did not take away the pillar of cloud by day, nor the pillar of fire by night, from before the people.*

These verses clearly reveal that the Israelites walked a long way traveling both day and night through a wilderness before crossing the Red Sea. Because the Red Sea crossing miracle happened several days after the Exodus, it couldn't have happened at the Suez finger of the Red Sea because Goshen is just 20 miles (32 km.) from the sea, a distance of just a few hours walk. Moreover, between Goshen and the believed traditional crossing place of the Red Sea is not a wilderness.

The Sinai Peninsula is a wilderness that would fit the biblical narrative of the Israelites traveling by day and by night before crossing the sea.

Research shows that a person could cross the Sinai Peninsula in 3 days traveling day and night at a normal walking pace of just 3 or so miles an hour.

Scripture also says that there were no feeble ones among them, and that God carried them supernaturally on eagle's wings during their exodus. These factors provide more evidence that the Israelites could have easily crossed the Sinai Peninsula and arrived at the Aqaba finger of the Red Sea at Nuweiba Beach.

Coral growth in the Red Sea by Nuweiba Beach

8. **There has been found in the Aqaba finger of the Red Sea at Nuweiba Beach amazing evidence of coral growth on objects that look like old chariot wheels, axles, etc. These same objects have also been found on the shore across from Nuweiba Beach on the Saudi Arabian side of the Red Sea.**

Coral doesn't grow in sandy areas and must have some object to grow on. The Red Sea is very sandy from Nuweiba Beach to the

Saudi Arabian shore, so there's no reason coral would grow in this area unless there were foreign objects for it to grow on.

9. **Nuweiba Beach is very large and could have easily accommodated the 3 million or so Israelites.**

   The beach at Nuweiba is large, flat, and sandy, a perfect place for the 2.5 to 3 million Israelites to camp.

10. **The ocean floor of the Red Sea by Nuweiba Beach gradually goes down and then gradually goes up to the shore of Saudi Arabia.**

    Just north or south of this area, there are deep impassable ravines on the ocean floor. The Nuweiba Beach location is the only place on the Aqaba finger of the Red Sea that would have allowed the Israelites to cross. It seems reasonable to suggest that God, in His

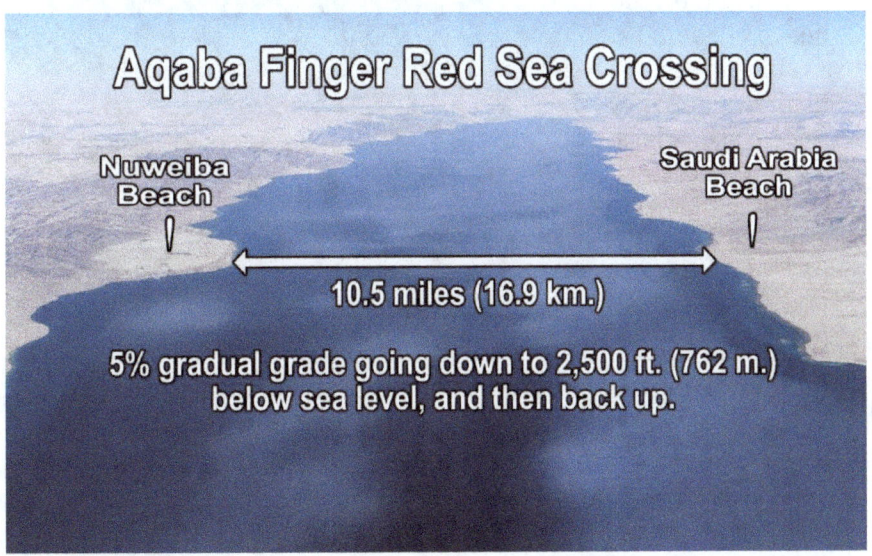

sovereignty, divinely created this sandy, gradual crossing place for the Israelites to use for this magnanimous miracle.

The maximum depth of the ocean floor at this crossing place is about 2,500 ft. deep (762 m.). This fits the biblical narrative that God divided the "mighty waters" of the sea.

Exodus 14:29: *But the sons of Israel walked on dry land through the **midst of the sea**, and the waters were **like a wall** to them on their right hand and on their left.*

Exodus 15:10: *You blew with Your wind, the sea covered them; They sank like lead in the **mighty waters**.*

Isaiah 51:10: *Was it not You who dried up the sea, the **waters of the great deep**; who made the **depths of the sea** a pathway for the redeemed to cross over?*

The shallow lakebeds and marshes by Egypt were certainly not waters of the **great deep**.

11. **Solomon referred to the Aqaba finger of the Red Sea, and archaeological discoveries have found two pillars he erected on each side of the Red Sea crossing.**

    1 Kings 9:26: *King Solomon also built a fleet of ships in Ezion-geber, which is near Eloth [modern-day Eilat] on the shore of the **Red Sea**, in the land of Edom.*

    At Nuweiba Beach, and on the beach of Saudi Arabia across from Nuweiba Beach, are pillars Solomon erected marking the crossing of the Red Sea by the Israelites.

    Solomon Pillar at Nuweiba Beach

12. **When the Israelites arrived at the location of Nuweiba Beach, they were certainly hemmed in, as Scripture says.**

    Exodus 14:1–3: *Then the Lord said to Moses, 2 "Tell the people of Israel to turn back and encamp in front of Pi-hahiroth, between Migdol **and the sea**, in front of Baal-zephon; you shall encamp facing it, **by the sea**. 3 For Pharaoh will say of the people of Israel, 'They are wandering in the land; the wilderness has **shut them in**.'"*

    The landscape at Nuweiba Beach is unique and mountainous and would fit the biblical narrative.

13. **As a result of being hemmed in and threatened by the Egyptian army, the Israelites cried out to Moses in anger and desperation.**

    Exodus 14:13–14: *But Moses said to the people, "Do not fear! Stand by and see the salvation of the Lord which He will accomplish for you today; for the Egyptians whom you have seen today, you will never see them again forever. 14 The Lord will fight for you while you keep silent."*

14. Then the hand of God performed one of the greatest miracles ever recorded in Scripture.

Exodus 14:15–31: *Then the Lord said to Moses, "Why are you crying out to Me? Tell the sons of Israel to go forward. 16 As for you, lift up your staff and stretch out your hand over the sea and divide it, and the sons of Israel shall go through the **midst of the sea** on dry land. 17 As for Me, behold, I will harden the hearts of the Egyptians so that they will go in after*

them; and I will be honored through Pharaoh and all his army, through his chariots and his horsemen. 18 Then the Egyptians will know that I am the Lord, when I am honored through Pharaoh, through his chariots and his horsemen."

19 The angel of God, who had been going before the camp of Israel, moved and went behind them; and the pillar of cloud moved from before them and stood behind them. 20 So it came between the camp of Egypt and the camp of Israel; and there was the cloud along with the darkness, yet it gave light at night. Thus, the one did not come near the other all night.

*21 Then Moses stretched out his hand over the sea; and the Lord swept the sea back by a strong east wind all night and turned the sea into dry land, so the waters were divided. 22 The sons of Israel went through the midst of the sea on the dry land, and the waters were **like a wall to them** on their right hand and on their left. 23 Then the Egyptians took up the pursuit, and all Pharaoh's horses, his chariots and his horsemen went in after them into the midst of the sea. 24 At the morning watch, the Lord looked down on the army of the Egyptians through the pillar of fire and cloud and brought the army of the Egyptians into confusion. 25 He caused their chariot wheels to swerve, and He made them drive with difficulty; so the*

Egyptians said, "Let us flee from Israel, for the Lord is fighting for them against the Egyptians."

26 Then the Lord said to Moses, "Stretch out your hand over the sea so that the waters may come back over the Egyptians, over their chariots and their horsemen." 27 So Moses stretched out his hand over the sea, and the sea returned to its normal state at daybreak, while the Egyptians were fleeing right into it; then the Lord overthrew the Egyptians in the **midst of the sea**. 28 The waters returned and covered the

Split Rock at Rephidim

chariots and the horsemen, even Pharaoh's entire army that had gone into the sea after them; not even one of them remained. 29 But the sons of Israel walked on dry land through **the midst of the sea**, and the **waters were like a wall** to them on their right hand and on their left.

30 Thus the Lord saved Israel that day from the hand of the Egyptians, and Israel saw the Egyptians dead on the seashore. 31 When Israel saw the great power which the Lord had used against the Egyptians, the people feared the Lord, and they believed in the Lord and in His servant Moses.

The entire Egyptian army drowned in the sea, and if the army was around 250,000, this couldn't have happened in the shallow marshes east of Egypt. So it had to occur in a wide and deep body of water.

15. **After crossing the Red Sea, the Bible says the Israelites then traveled to Mount Sinai. Does the location of Mount Sinai in Saudi Arabia (biblical Midian) fit the biblical narrative?**

When Moses fled to Egypt to save his life, Scripture says he went to Midian.

Exodus 2:15: *When Pharaoh heard of this matter, he tried to kill*

Negev & Southern Israel Sites

*Moses. But Moses fled from the presence of Pharaoh and settled in the **land of Midian**, and he sat down by a well.*

Midian is in Saudi Arabia, not in the Sinai Peninsula.

Galatians 4:25: *Now this Hagar is **Mount Sinai in Arabia** and corresponds to the present Jerusalem, for she is in slavery with her children.*

When God appeared to Moses in a burning bush at Mount Sinai, God said that Moses would bring the people out of Egypt and worship at the same Mount Sinai (also known as Mount Horeb). Moses was in Midian when this event occurred, so it seems very convincing that Mount Sinai is in Midian.

Exodus 3:1–2: *Now Moses was pasturing the flock of Jethro his father-in-law, the priest of **Midian**; and he led the flock to the west side of the wilderness and came to **Horeb, the mountain of God**. 2 The angel of the Lord appeared to him in a blazing fire from the midst of a bush; and he looked, and behold, the bush was burning with fire, yet the bush was not consumed.*

Mount Sinai with dark top

Exodus 3:12: *And He said, "Certainly I will be with you, and this shall be the sign to you that it is I who have sent you: when you have brought the people out of Egypt, you shall worship God **at this mountain**."*

16. **Evidence from the places the Israelites camped on their way from the Red Sea crossing to Mount Sinai supports Mount Sinai's location in Midian.**

    Location of Elim

    Exodus 15:27: *Then they came to **Elim** where there were twelve springs of water and seventy date palms, and they camped there beside the waters.*

The location of Elim has been identified in Saudi Arabia, about 26 miles (42 km.) south of the Red Sea crossing.

Caves of Jethro

There are caves named after Jethro the Midianite (Moses' father-in-law) that have been found by the route the Israelites took from the Red Sea crossing to Mount Sinai. This shows that Jethro lived in this area and that it was the land of Midian at that time.

Split Rock at Rephidim

Exodus 17:1: *Then all the congregation of the sons of Israel journeyed by stages from the wilderness of Sin, according to the command of the Lord, and camped at* **Rephidim**, *and there was no water for the people to drink.*

Exodus 17:6: *Behold, I will stand before you there on the rock at Horeb; and you shall strike the rock, and* **water will come out of it**, *that the people may drink."*

This rock at Rephidim is believed to have been found. It is a large rock that is split from top to bottom and shows water grooves where massive amounts of water ran down from it.

17. **Evidence for the location of Mount Sinai in Midian.**

Mount Sinai in Midian (Saudi Arabia) has a blackened and burnt top, which fits the biblical narrative.

Exodus 19:18: *Now Mount Sinai was all in smoke because the Lord descended upon it in fire; and its smoke ascended*

Golden Calf altar at Mt. Sinai

like the smoke of a furnace, and the whole mountain quaked violently.

At the base of Mount Sinai in Midian is an altar Moses erected, 12 stones Moses erected by the altar, an altar to a Golden Calf with paintings of calves and animals, a rock painting of a menorah, a cave where Elijah could have stayed, and archaeological findings.

Today, sections of the area and the mountain are fenced off by the Saudi Arabian government and designated as archeological sites. However, there are no excavations permitted on them at this time.

18. Other Evidence from ancient historians.

Several Jewish documents dating 600 years before Christ locate Mount Sinai in Midian, and Philo and Josephus (Jewish historians) also located Mount Sinai in Midian of Arabia.

Faith Lesson from the Exodus, Red Sea Crossing, and Mount Sinai

1. The deliverance of the Israelites from Egypt was done to show several deep theological truths:
   - To show God's power and glory (He is above all gods and is the only true God).
   - To be a foreshadow of salvation and deliverance (God can save and deliver us as He did the Israelites).
   - To teach His chosen people how to follow and obey Him.
   - To show his power and glory to the other nations.
2. The important thing to realize is that the location of the events of the Exodus, Red Sea crossing, and Mount Sinai are not the determining factor for whether the Bible is true. However, this evidence does strengthen our faith to know the events spoken of in Scripture are true and historical.
3. The miracles surrounding the Exodus, Red Sea crossing, and Mount Sinai are some of the greatest miracles found in Scripture.
4. All of this should inspire us to trust and obey God more fully.

Journal/Notes:

Hebron

Location

1. The city of Hebron is set in the Judean Mountains about 20 miles (32 km.) south of Jerusalem.
2. Hebron stands 3,000 ft. (914 m.) above sea level, making it the highest city in Israel.
3. While there have been tensions in the past between Israelis and Arabs, the Cave of the Patriarchs and Tel Hebron (Tel Rumeida) is protected by Israeli forces, and around 250,000 tourists visit Hebron annually.

Historical Background

1. Hebron is one of the most popular places in the Bible, being mentioned 72 times.
2. It was inhabited by the Canaanites before Abraham and the Israelites arrived.
3. Hebron is the beginning place and roots of the nation of Israel. The promises and covenants God made with Abraham and his descendants happened here or nearby. These promises would also have wide-reaching implications and include all the nations of the earth.
4. All the patriarchs and their wives, except Rachel, one of Jacob's wives, are buried in Hebron.
5. Located in Hebron is Machpelah, the Cave of the Patriarchs.
    - Abraham purchased the cave and the adjoining field at full market price as a burial place for his family some 3,700 years ago.
    - The Cave of the Patriarchs building is the second holiest site in

Judaism (after the Western Wall in Jerusalem) and is also sacred to Christians and Muslims.
- In the cave are the tombs of Abraham and Sarah, Isaac and Rebekah, and Jacob and Leah.
- King Herod built a massive wall around the cave around 20 BC to preserve it and establish a memorial place for the Jews. He used the same style of stones as he did for the Temple Mount walls in Jerusalem.
- This is the only building in Israel that has remained intact and undamaged since it was built.
- It was used over the centuries as a church by the Byzantine and Crusaders, then as a mosque by the Muslims.

Machpelah: Cave of the Patriarchs

- The Byzantines erected a small basilica with a roof over part of the interior, and the Crusaders built the roof that exists today that covers the entire building.
- Today, the Cave of the Patriarch building is shared by the Jews and Muslims. On one side of the building is a synagogue and on the other side is a mosque.
- The tombs of the patriarchs are under the foundation of the building, but their memorial monuments are visible in the building on the first floor.

Places of Interest

1. Cave of the Patriarchs (Machpelah)
   - Jewish Synagogue
   - Mosque
   - Tombs of the Patriarchs and Matriarchs
2. Tel Hebron (Tel Rumeida)
   - Abraham's Well

- Ancient Stairs
- Tomb of Jesse and Ruth (King David's father and great grandmother)
- Old Olive Trees
- Ancient City Walls
- Mikvahs
- Ancient Synagogue
- New Excavations

3. Oaks of Mamre

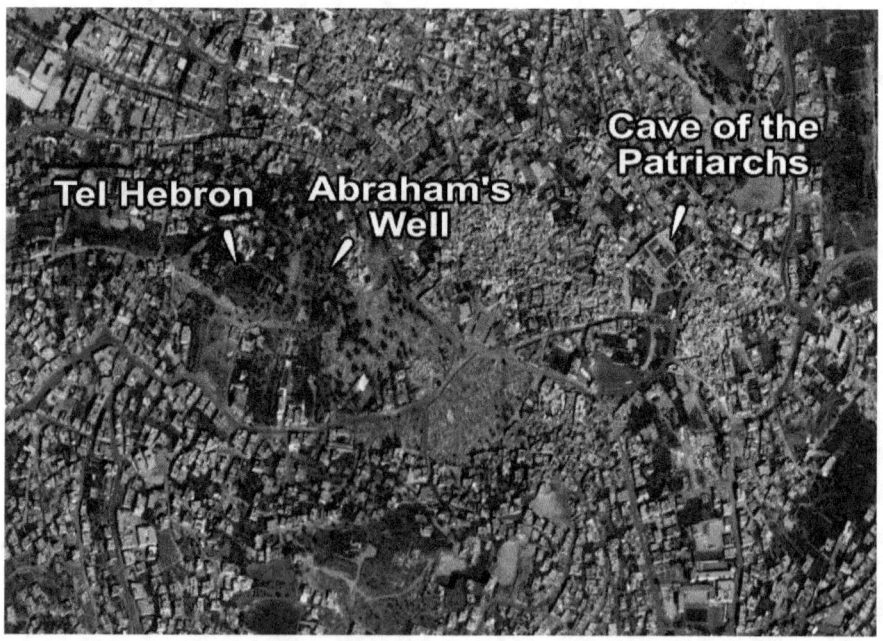

Hebron in the Bible

1. **After God affirmed His covenant with Abraham in Hebron, he built an altar to the Lord and lived there.**

   Genesis 13:17–18: *Arise, walk about the land through its length and breadth; for I will give it to you. 18 Then Abram moved his tent and came and dwelt by the oaks of Mamre, which are in **Hebron**, and there he built an altar to the Lord.*

2. **At Hebron, Abraham learned in a dream that his descendants would spend 400 years as slaves in Egypt.**

Negev & Southern Israel Sites

Genesis 15:12–14: *Now when the sun was going down, a deep sleep fell upon Abram; and behold, terror and great darkness fell upon him. 13 God said to Abram, "Know for certain that your descendants will be strangers in a land that is not theirs, where they will be enslaved and oppressed four hundred years. 14 But I will also judge the nation whom they will serve, and afterward, they will come out with many possessions."*

3. **At Hebron, Ismael was born to Abraham and Sarah's handmaid, Hagar (Gen. 16:4).**

4. **Near Hebron, God made a covenant with Abraham that he would be "the ancestor of a multitude of nations."**

   Genesis 17:1–8: *When Abram was ninety-nine years old the L*ORD *appeared to Abram and said to him, "I am God Almighty; walk before me, and be blameless, 2 that I may make my covenant between me and you, and may multiply you greatly." 3 Then Abram fell on his face. And God said to him, 4 "Behold, my covenant is with you, and you shall be the father of a multitude of nations. 5 No longer shall your name be called Abram, but your name shall be Abraham, for I have made you the father of a multitude of nations. 6 I will make you exceedingly fruitful, and I will make you into nations, and kings shall come from you. 7 And I will establish my covenant between me and you and your offspring after you throughout their generations for an everlasting covenant, to be God to you and to your offspring after you. 8 And I will give to you and to your offspring after you the land of your sojournings, all the land of Canaan, for an everlasting possession, and I will be their God."*

   Abraham's Well

5. **At Hebron, Abraham offered hospitality to three servant angels of God and received the promise of a son.**

   Genesis 18:10–14: *They said to him, "Where is Sarah your wife?" And he said, "She is in the tent." 10 The L*ORD *said, "I will surely return to you about this time next year, and Sarah your wife shall* have a son." And Sarah was listening at the tent door behind him. 11 Now Abraham and Sarah were old, advanced in years. The way of women had ceased to be with Sarah. 12 So Sarah laughed to herself, saying, "After I am worn out, and my lord is old, shall I have pleasure?" 13 The LORD said to Abraham, "Why did Sarah laugh and say, 'Shall I indeed bear a child, now that I am old?' 14 Is anything too hard for the LORD? At the appointed time I will return to you, about this time next year, and Sarah shall have a son."

Ancient synagogue at Hebron

6. **At Hebron, Abraham bought the Cave of Machpelah as a burial place for his wife, Sarah, and his family.**

    Genesis 23:19: *After this, Abraham buried Sarah his wife in the cave of the field at Machpelah facing Mamre (that is, **Hebron**) in the land of Canaan.*

7. **Later, Abraham, Isaac, Rebecca, Jacob, and Leah would be buried in the Cave of Machpelah as well.**

8. **Jacob returned to Hebron after he had sojourned in Paddan-aram.**

    Genesis 35:27: *Jacob came to his father Isaac at Mamre of Kiriath-arba (that is, **Hebron**), where Abraham and Isaac had sojourned.*

9. **Joseph was sent from Hebron to Shechem, where he would be sold into slavery and taken to Egypt.**

    Genesis 37:14: *Then he said to him, "Go now and see about the welfare of your brothers and the welfare of the flock, and bring word back to me." So he sent him from the valley of **Hebron**, and he came to Shechem.*

10. **Nearby to Hebron, two of the spies who researched the Promised Land returned with a large cluster of grapes.**

    Numbers 13:21–23: *So the men explored the land from the Desert of Zin to the border of Hamath. 22 They went through the Negev and came to **Hebron**, where Ahiman, Sheshai, and Talmai lived. They are* descendants of Anak. (Hebron was built seven years before Zoan in Egypt.) 23 When they came to the Eshcol Valley, they cut off a branch with **only one bunch of grapes** on it. They carried it on a pole between two of them.

11. **Hebron was given to Caleb as an inheritance for his faithfulness to the Lord.**

    Joshua 14:13–14: *So Joshua blessed him and gave **Hebron** to Caleb the son of Jephunneh for an inheritance. 14 Therefore, Hebron became the inheritance of Caleb, the son of Jephunneh the Kenizzite until this day, because he followed the Lord God of Israel fully.*

    Tombs of Jesse and Ruth

12. **Samson carried the gates of Gaza 35 miles (55 km.) up to Hebron (Judg. 16:1–3).**
13. **David was anointed king in Hebron and reigned here for 7 ½ years (2 Sam. 2:1–4, 11).**

Faith Lesson from Hebron

1. God confirmed His promises and covenants with Abraham at Hebron and fulfilled them all. Do we believe and embrace the promises of God?
2. Caleb was one of the faithful spies who received Hebron as a reward. Are we faithful like Caleb, and do we have our hope placed in our eternal home in heaven as our reward?
3. David was anointed king in Hebron because he was a person after God's own heart. Do we love the Lord like David, and are we desiring to serve Him in significant ways as David did?

Journal/Notes:

Negev & Southern Israel Biblical Sites Guide

Inn of the Good Samaritan

Location

1. The Inn of the Good Samaritan is located about 8.5 miles (13.5 km.) east of Jerusalem on Hwy. 1 and about 6.5 (10.5 km.) west of Jericho.
2. The Inn is about halfway between Jerusalem and Jericho on an ancient road that linked traffic from the Jordan Valley to Jerusalem and the coastal towns of the Mediterranean Ocean.

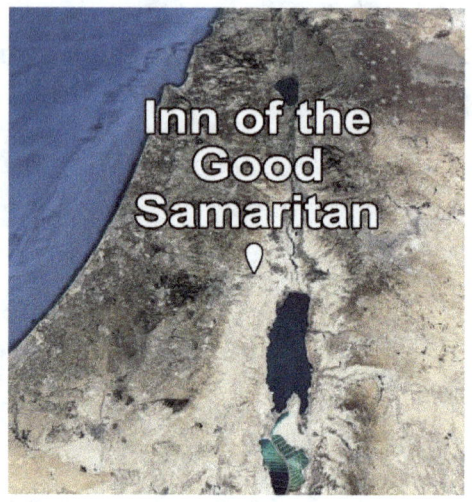

3. The famous story of the Good Samaritan took place on this road.

Historical Background

1. Interestingly, Jesus used real places and people in the story of the Good Samaritan, i.e., road, Jerusalem, Jericho, robbers, Samaritans, priests, Levites, and the Inn. Therefore, the possibility exists that the story was actually a real event that had happened.
2. The ancient road connecting the Jordan Valley to Jerusalem and beyond had an elevation difference of 3,400 ft. (1,036 m.). Jericho is at 800 ft. (244 m.) below sea level, and Jerusalem is at 2,600 ft. (792 m.) above sea level.
3. It was a dangerous road that was desolate in places, steep, curvy, with crooks, crannies, and caves where bandits and robbers could hide out and get away easily in the desert. It also lacked police protection in many places.
4. It was about 15 miles (24 km.) between Jerusalem and Jericho.
5. Around 12,000 priests and Levites lived in Jericho who used this road whenever they were summoned to serve in the temple in Jerusalem.
6. The rocky desert terrain around the Inn of the Good Samaritan was notorious for robbers. The local name for the area is Ma'ale Adummim, which means red rocks. It's believed the name was

derived from the limestone stained red by iron oxide, but it's also believed its name is due to the amount of blood that was spilled here by bandits and robbers.

7. Jesus and His disciples would have used this road repeatedly as they traveled between Jerusalem and Jericho.
8. The Inn of the Good Samaritan.
    - Although it's not certain that the inn Jesus mentioned in the story of the Good Samaritan was a real place, a site was proposed in the early Christian centuries as a place to commemorate this event. Today, it's called the Inn of the Good Samaritan.

    Inn of the Good Samaritan

    - The site was inhabited in the Hellenistic and Roman periods, and remains from the 1st century BC to the 1st century AD were discovered during the excavations of the Inn.
    - In the 6th century, a Byzantine church and monastery with pilgrim accommodations were erected on the site of what was probably some sort of travelers' hostel before the time of Jesus.
    - Later, the Crusaders built a fortress on a nearby hill to protect pilgrims against robbers.
    - The remains of the monastery later became an Ottoman Inn.
    - In the 1800s, the Ottomans built a rectangular structure over the ruins of the southern wall of the Crusader Fortress.
    - The current museum at this site was opened in 2009.

Places of Interest

1. Byzantine Church
2. Museum (has many mosaics and artifacts from around Israel)
3. Caves 1 and 2
4. Crusader Fortress

5. Hwy. 1
6. Jericho
7. Jerusalem
8. Ancient Road from Jericho to Jerusalem.
9. Wadi Qelt

The Story of the Good Samaritan in the Bible

1. **A lawyer (student of Scripture) tested Jesus regarding what a person had to do to receive eternal life.**

   Luke 10:25–28: *And a lawyer stood up and put Him to the test, saying, "Teacher, **what shall I do to inherit eternal life**?" 26 And He said to him, "What is written in the Law? How does it read to you?" 27 And he answered, "You shall love the Lord your God with all your heart, and with all your soul, and with all your strength, and with all your mind [Deut. 6:5]; and your neighbor as yourself [Lev. 19:18]." 28 And He said to him, "You have answered correctly; do this and you will live."*

2. **Attempting to justify himself, the lawyer asked a follow-up question about what the term "neighbor" meant.**

   Luke 10:29: *And He said to him, "You have answered correctly; do this and you will live." But wishing to justify himself, he said to Jesus, "And who is my **neighbor**?"*

3. **To illustrate who our neighbor is, Jesus told the story of the Good Samaritan.**

   Luke 10:30–34: *Jesus replied and said, "A man was **going down** from Jerusalem to Jericho, and fell among robbers, and they stripped him and beat him, and went away leaving him half dead. 31 And by chance a priest was going down on that road, and when he saw him, he passed by on the other side. 32 Likewise, a Levite also, when he came to the place and saw him,*

Inn of the Good Samaritan

passed by on the other side. 33 But a Samaritan who was on a journey, came upon him; and when he saw him, he felt compassion, 34 and came to him and bandaged up his wounds, pouring oil and wine on them; and he put him on his own beast, and brought him to an inn and took care of him."

- The priests were the spiritual leaders and oversaw the temple.
- The Levites were servants in the temple.
- Samaritans were unfaithful Jews who intermarried with foreign unbelievers and established their own religion.
- The Samaritans were despised and rejected by the Jews and considered unclean.
- The Samaritans, likewise, despised the Jews and had few dealings with them.
- Under the Hasmonean Reign (167-63 BC), the Jews destroyed the temple and city of the Samaritans in Shechem.
- Any traveler from Samaria would have been regarded as an alien in Judea.

Luke 10:35–37: *On the next day, he took out two denarii and gave them to the innkeeper and said, "Take care of him; and whatever more you spend, when I return, I will repay*

Inn of the Good Samaritan

*you." 36 Which of these three do you think proved to be a neighbor to the man who fell into the robbers' hands? 37 And he said, "The one who showed mercy toward him." Then Jesus said to him, "**Go and do the same**."*

- A denarius was about a day's wage. Today, it would be around $200 dollars for an average worker. The Samaritan gave the innkeeper two denarii for a total of $400 dollars.
- The Good Samaritan was willing to spend even more money on the hurt man, meaning that what he had already given was just a start.

Faith Lesson from the Good Samaritan

1. Our neighbor is anyone with a genuine need whom we find in our path.
2. The wounded man the Samaritan helped was not a family member, a friend, or an acquaintance; he was a total stranger.
3. The Samaritan spent a large sum of money to help heal the wounded man with no expectation or guarantee of being repaid.
4. It's not what we see but what we do that makes us a neighbor.
5. Jesus emphasized that it's not just what we believe that matters, but what we do that shows we are truly saved.
6. While we should help the wounded with physical needs, we should also help the wounded with their spiritual needs as well. The greatest need everyone has is salvation. Do we share our faith and give the greatest gift possible to those in need spiritually?

7. We should keep in mind that not every want or need others might have are legitimate.
8. God doesn't want us to reward wrong motives and laziness.

    2 Thessalonians 3:10–11: *For even when we were with you, we used to give you this order:* ***if anyone is not willing to work, then he is not to eat****, either. 11 For we hear that some among you are leading an **undisciplined life, doing no work at all**, but acting like busybodies.*

Journal/Notes:

Jericho

Location

1. Jericho is in the Jordan Valley about 8 miles (13 km.) north of the Dead Sea and about 15 miles (24 km.) east of Jerusalem.
2. It's situated at 800 ft. (244 m.) below sea level, making it the lowest city in the world.
3. Jericho claims to be the oldest city in the world that has been continuously inhabited.
4. Its name means "City of Palms."
5. It was located at the crossroads of two main travel routes. It had a north-south route that ran through the Jordan Valley, and an east-west route that connected the east side of the Jordan River with Jerusalem, the Samaritan cities, and the coastal plain cities of the Mediterranean Sea.
6. It has a year-round climate with lots of sun.
7. Tel Jericho is also known today as Tell Es-Sultan.

Historical Background

1. Jericho was a well-fortified Canaanite city before the arrival of the Israelites.
2. It's an ancient city with about 6 thousand years of history.
3. Archaeologists have uncovered 23 levels of civilizations at Tel Jericho.
4. The city was fortified with double walls.
    - The walls were constructed of large stones at the base and mud bricks continuing upwards.
    - The exterior wall's stone base was about 10–12 ft. high (3 m.), and the mud-brick wall on top of it was another 20–25 ft. tall (7

m.), for a total of around 35 ft. (11 m.).
- The inner wall was constructed the same way; only it rose even higher than the exterior wall for a total height of around 50 ft. (15 m.).
- The width of the walls were around 8 ft. (2.5 m.) wide each, and people lived between them (Josh. 2:15).
- These double walls were enormous and overwhelming in size and strength.
5. Jericho was given by Marc Antony (Roman general under Julius Caesar) to Cleopatra (Pharaoh of Egypt) as a wedding gift in 36 BC.
6. King Herod built a winter palace in Jericho around 20 BC and would later die there as well.
7. During the Byzantine period, homes and churches were built in the area.
8. During the Crusader period, the town was moved about a mile (1.6 km.) southeast of Tel Jericho.

Places of Interest in General

1. Tel Jericho
2. Mount of Temptation Monastery
3. Jericho Cable Cars – Access to Mount of Temptation Monastery.
4. Hisham's Palace – 8th century Muslim Palace.
5. Modern Jericho
6. Shittim – Place the Israelites camped on the east side of the Jordan River before entering the Promised Land.
7. Camp Gilgal – Place the Israelites camped after entering the Promised Land.
8. Zacchaeus Tree
9. Herod's Palace
10. St. George's Monastery – Hanging monastery with Cave of Elijah.
11. Baptismal Site of Jesus
12. Jordan River
13. Dead Sea

Places of Interest at Tel Jericho

1. Elisha's Spring – Tourist viewing place.
2. Tower
3. Walls
4. Ancient Homes
5. Burn & Ash Layers
6. Palace
7. Building
8. Neolithic Tower
9. Byzantine Homes
10. Walls
11. Preserved Wall and Homes – This area is likely where Rahab lived as it was spared in the destruction by the Lord.
12. Elisha's Spring – Main source of water for Jericho.

Negev & Southern Israel Sites

Archaeological Evidence at Tel Jericho that Proves the Bible is True

1. Retaining Walls
2. Fallen Mudbrick Walls
3. Preserved section of the wall where Rahab likely lived.
4. Burn Layer
5. Burnt full jars of barley.
6. The battle was short, as shown in the archaeology.
7. The battle took place in the Spring during the barley harvest.
8. Discovered abandonment layer due to Joshua's curse on Jericho.
9. Jericho was rebuilt by the Israelites during the time of King Ahab, according to Joshua's prophecy.
10. Israelite occupation layer.

Jericho in the Bible

1. **Rahab the prostitute, who hid the Israelite Spies, was from Jericho.**

   Joshua 2:1: *And Joshua the son of Nun sent two men secretly from Shittim as spies, saying, "Go, view the land, especially **Jericho**." And they went and came into the house of a prostitute whose name was **Rahab** and lodged there.*

   Joshua 2:8–15: *Before the men lay down, she came up to them on the roof, 9 and said to the men, "I know that the Lord has given you the land, and that the fear of you has fallen upon us, and that all the inhabitants of the land melt away before you. 10 For we have heard how the Lord dried up the water of the Red Sea before you when you came out of Egypt, and what you did to the two kings of the Amorites who were beyond the Jordan, to Sihon and Og, whom you devoted to destruction. 11 And as soon as we heard it, our hearts melted, and there was no spirit left in any man because of you, for the Lord your God, he is God in the heavens above and on the earth beneath. 12 Now then, please swear to me by the Lord that, as I have dealt kindly with you, you also will deal kindly with my father's house, and give me a sure sign 13 that you will save alive my father and mother, my brothers and sisters, and all who belong to them, and deliver our lives from death." 14 And the men said to her, "Our life for yours even to death! If you do not tell this business of ours, then when the Lord gives us the land we will deal kindly and faithfully with you." 15 Then she let them down by a rope through the window, for her house was built into the city wall, so that **she lived in the wall**.*

   Walls where Rahab might have lived

2. **The Children of Israel crossed the Jordan River near Jericho.**

   Joshua 3:14–16: *So when the people set out from their tents to pass over the Jordan with the priests bearing the ark of the covenant before the people, 15 and as soon as those bearing the ark had come as far as the Jordan, and the feet of the priests bearing the ark were*

Negev & Southern Israel Sites

*dipped in the brink of the water (now the Jordan overflows all its banks throughout the time of harvest), 16 the waters coming down from above stood and rose up in a heap very far away, at Adam, the city that is beside Zarethan, and those flowing down toward the Sea of the Arabah, the Salt Sea, were completely cut off. And the people passed over opposite **Jericho**.*

3. **The Israelites camped at Camp Gilgal after entering the Promised Land.**

   Joshua 4:19: *The people came up out of the Jordan on the tenth day of the first month, and they encamped at **Gilgal on the east border of Jericho**.*

4. **The Israelites celebrated the Passover after crossing the Jordan River.**

   Joshua 5:10: *While the sons of Israel camped at Gilgal they celebrated the Passover on the evening of the fourteenth day of the month on the desert plains of Jericho.*

5. **Jericho was the first city captured by the Israelites when they entered the Promised Land.**

   Joshua 6:1–5: *Now **Jericho** was shut up inside and outside because of the people of Israel. None went out, and none came in. 2 And the Lord said to Joshua, "See, I have given **Jericho** into your hand, with its king and mighty men of valor. 3 You shall march around the city, all the men of war going around the city once. Thus shall you do for six days. 4 Seven priests shall bear seven trumpets of rams' horns before the ark. On the seventh day you shall march around the city seven times, and the priests shall blow the trumpets. 5 And when they make a long blast with the ram's horn, when you hear the sound of the trumpet, then all the people shall shout with a great shout, and the wall of the city will fall down flat, and the people **shall go up**, everyone straight before him."*

Jericho had double-walled fortification

   Joshua 6:15–16: *On the seventh day they rose early, at the dawn of* day, and marched around the city in the same manner seven times. It was only on that day that they marched around the city seven times. 16 And at the seventh time, when the priests had blown the trumpets, Joshua said to the people, "Shout, for the Lord has given you the city."

Walls of Jericho

6. **The mud-brick walls of Jericho fell flat (beneath themselves) and formed a ramp.**

   Joshua 6:20–22: *So the people shouted, and the trumpets were blown. As soon as the people heard the sound of the trumpet, the people shouted a great shout, and the wall fell down flat, so that the people went up into the city, every man straight before him, and they captured the city. 21 Then they devoted all in the city to destruction, both men and women, young and old, oxen, sheep, and donkeys, with the edge of the sword. 22 But to the two men who had spied out the land, Joshua said, "Go into the prostitute's house and bring out from there the woman and all who belong to her, as you swore to her."*

7. **Joshua burned the city of Jericho with fire. Burn layer found throughout the tel.**

   Walls of Jericho fell flat towards the outside of the city

   Joshua 6:24: *And they burned the city with fire, and everything in it.*

8. **Joshua cursed Jericho, and it laid abandoned for many centuries.**

This formed an abandonment layer that can be seen today.

Joshua 6:26: *Then Joshua made them take an oath at that time, saying, "Cursed before the Lord is the man who rises up and builds this city Jericho; with the loss of his firstborn he will lay its foundation, and with the loss of his youngest son he will set up its gates."*

9. **Jericho was rebuilt during the time of King Ahab around 875 BC.**

    1 Kings 16:34: *In his days Hiel the Bethelite rebuilt Jericho; he laid its foundations with the loss of Abiram his firstborn, and set up its gates with the loss of his youngest son Segub, in accordance with the word of the Lord, which He spoke by Joshua the son of Nun.*

10. **The prophets, Elijah and Elisha, traversed in Jericho often.**

    2 Kings 2:4: *Elijah said to him, "Elisha, please stay here, for the LORD has sent me to **Jericho**." But he said, "As the LORD lives, and as you yourself live, I will not leave you." So they came to **Jericho**.*

11. **Elisha healed the water source of Jericho.**

    Elisha's Spring

    2 Kings 2:19–22: *Now the men of the city said to Elisha, "Behold, the situation of this city is pleasant, as my lord sees, but the water is bad, and the land is unfruitful." 20 He said, "Bring me a new bowl, and put salt in it." So they brought it to him. 21 Then he went to the spring of water and threw salt in it and said, "Thus says the LORD, I have healed this water; from now*

on neither death nor miscarriage shall come from it." 22 So the water has been healed to this day, according to the word that Elisha spoke.

12. The miracle of a blind man healed by Jesus occurred in Jericho.

Luke 18:35–43: *As he [Jesus] drew near to **Jericho**, a blind man was sitting by the roadside begging. 36 And hearing a crowd going by, he inquired what this meant. 37 They told him, "Jesus of Nazareth is passing by." 38 And he cried out, "Jesus, Son of David, have mercy on me!" 39 And those who were in front rebuked him, telling him to be silent. But he cried out all the more, "Son of David, have mercy on me!" 40 And Jesus stopped and commanded him to be brought to him. And when he came near, he asked him, 41 "What do you want me to do for you?" He said, "Lord, let me recover my sight." 42 And Jesus said to him, "Recover your sight; your faith has made you well." 43 And immediately he recovered his sight and followed him, glorifying God. And all the people, when they saw it, gave praise to God.*

13. Zacchaeus, the Tax Collector, was from Jericho.

Luke 19:1–10: *He [Jesus] entered **Jericho** and was passing through. 2 And there was a man named Zacchaeus. He was a chief tax collector and was rich. 3 And he was seeking to see who Jesus was, but on*

Tel Jericho

account of the crowd he could not, because he was small of stature. 4 So he ran on ahead and climbed up into a sycamore tree to see him, for he was about to pass that way. 5 And when Jesus came to the place, he looked up and said to him, "Zacchaeus, hurry and come down, for I must stay at your house today." 6 So he hurried and came down and received him joyfully. 7 And when they saw it, they all grumbled, "He has gone in to be the guest of a man who is a sinner." 8 And Zacchaeus stood and said to the Lord, "Behold, Lord, the half of my goods I give to the poor. And if I have defrauded anyone of anything, I restore it fourfold." 9 And Jesus said to him, "Today salvation has come to this house, since he also is a son of Abraham. 10 For the Son of Man came to seek and to save the lost."

14. **The famous story of the Good Samaritan happened on the route from Jericho to Jerusalem (Luke 10:25-37).**

Faith Lesson from Jericho

1. The crumbling of the walls of Jericho by the shout of the Israelites proves to be one of the greatest miracles in the Bible. Do we believe God can crumble the obstacles in our lives today as well?
2. Rahab was a sinner who chose to fear the Lord and turn to Him. She was welcomed into the Jewish faith and became part of the lineage of Christ, along with Ruth the Moabitess.

   Matthew 1:5-6: *And Salmon the father of Boaz by* **Rahab**, *and Boaz the father of Obed by* **Ruth**, *and Obed the father of Jesse, 6 and Jesse the father of David the king.*

   Amazingly, in the genealogy of Christ, two generations in a row include foreign women who were saved by grace through faith and welcomed into the Jewish faith.
3. The lives of Rahab and Ruth illustrate that salvation has always been and always will be open to anyone willing to listen to God's call of salvation.
4. Jesus healed a blind man in Jericho because of his persevering faith. What about us? What kind of faith do we have in Christ? Do we give up easily, or do we persevere?
5. Zacchaeus, the Tax Collector, was another outsider who was willing to embrace Christ's love and offer of salvation. Jericho resounds with examples of outsiders who were rejected by others but sought out by God. Do we believe God loves outsiders today, and do we welcome them into our lives and churches?

Journal/Notes:

Jordan River Overview

Location

1. The Jordan River begins at Mount Hermon in the northernmost part of Israel, flows into the Sea of Galilee, and then out and down to the Dead Sea.
2. The lower part of the river has the lowest elevation of any river in the world.
3. It's the border between Israel and Jordan for much of its length.
4. Today, because of the high demands of water by both Israel and Jordan, little water makes it to the Dead Sea area.

Historical Background

1. The Jordan River is mentioned over 180 times in the Bible.
2. It is the main River in Israel, supplying much of the country with water.
3. Its total winding length is about 125 miles (200 km.).
4. The meaning of "Jordan" in Hebrew is "descend." This is true of the Jordan River as it literally descends thousands of feet from its inception to its ending, and all but the beginning part is below sea level.
5. However, there's a deeper spiritual meaning to the word. In the same way we must physically descend to access the Jordan River's waters, we must descend and humble ourselves before we can ascend spiritually. This concept is seen in many of the miracles that happened in and around its shores.

Places of Interest

1. Mount Hermon – Rises to around 9,232 ft. (2,813 m.) above sea level and supplies the Jordan River with most of its water.

Negev & Southern Israel Sites

2. Hermon Stream Nature Reserve – Beginning area of the Jordan River.
3. Jordan River View – Nice viewing place where the river is wide and calm.
4. Sea of Galilee – The Jordan River flows into and out of the Sea of Galilee.
5. Yardenit Baptismal Site – Located just south of the Sea of Galilee. It's a popular place where many pilgrims get baptized in the Jordan River.
6. Adam – Place the waters of the Jordan backed up to when the Israelites crossed the river (20 miles, 32 km. above crossing).
7. Baptismal Site of Jesus – Located across from Jericho, this is the believed place where Jesus was baptized. It's also a popular place where many people get baptized today as well.
8. Crossing of the Jordan River by the Israelites – Located nearby to the Baptismal Site of Jesus.
9. Camp Gilgal
10. Jericho
11. Dead Sea

Jordan River in the Bible

1. **Abraham entered the Promised Land through the gateway of the Jordan River Valley when he first journeyed from Ur of the Chaldeans (Gen. 12:1–9).**

2. **When Abraham and Lot divided their possessions, Lot chose to settle in the lower part of the Jordan River Valley.**

   Genesis 13:10: *And Lot lifted up his eyes and saw that the **Jordan Valley** was well watered everywhere like the garden of the LORD, like the land of Egypt, in the direction of Zoar. (This was before the LORD destroyed Sodom and Gomorrah.)*

3. **Before entering the Promised Land, the Israelites camped on the east side of the Jordan River, opposite Jericho.**

   Joshua 3:1: *Then Joshua rose early in the morning, and they set out from Shittim. And they came to the **Jordan**, he and all the people of Israel, and lodged there before they passed over.*

4. **The Israelites crossed the Jordan River on dry ground as God miraculously parted the waters.**

   Joshua 3:14–17: *So when the people set out from their tents to pass over the **Jordan** with the priests bearing the ark of the covenant before the people, 15 and as soon as those bearing the ark had come as far as the **Jordan**, and the **feet of the priests** bearing the ark were dipped in the brink*

   Hermon Springs Nature Reserve (Caesarea Philippi)

   *of the water (**now the Jordan overflows all its banks throughout the time of harvest**), 16 the waters coming down from above stood and rose up in a heap very far away, at Adam [20 miles, 32 km. north], the city that is beside Zarethan, and those flowing down toward the Sea of the Arabah, the Salt Sea, were completely cut off. And the people passed over opposite Jericho. 17 Now the priests bearing the ark of the covenant of the Lord stood firmly on dry ground **in the midst of the Jordan**, and all Israel was passing over on dry ground until all the nation finished passing over the **Jordan**.*

Negev & Southern Israel Sites

5. Naaman, the Leper, was healed in the Jordan River by the Prophet Elisha.

2 Kings 5:10–14: *And Elisha sent a messenger to him, saying, "Go and wash in the **Jordan** seven times, and your flesh shall be restored, and you shall be clean." 11 But Naaman was angry and went away, saying, "Behold, I thought that he would surely come out to me and stand and call upon the name of the LORD his God, and wave his hand over the place and cure the leper. 12 Are not Abana and Pharpar, the rivers of Damascus, better than all the waters of Israel? Could I not wash in them and be clean?" So he turned and went away in a rage. 13 But his servants came near and said to him, "My father, it is a great word the prophet has spoken to you; will you not do it? Has he actually said to you, 'Wash, and be clean?'" 14 So he went down and dipped himself seven times in the **Jordan**, according to the word of the man of God, and his flesh was restored like the flesh of a little child, and he was clean.*

Jordan River north of the Sea of Galilee

6. Elijah parted the waters of the Jordan with his cloak.

2 Kings 2:6–8: *Then Elijah said to him, "Please stay here, for the Lord has sent me to the Jordan." But he said, "As the Lord lives, and as you yourself live, I will not leave you." So the two of them went on. 7 Fifty men of the sons of the prophets also went and stood at some distance from them, as they both were standing by the **Jordan**. 8 Then Elijah took his cloak and rolled it up and struck the water, and the water was parted to the one side and to the other, till the two of them could go over on dry ground.*

7. Elisha made the head of an ax float at the Jordan River.

2 Kings 6:1–7: *Now the sons of the prophets said to Elisha, "See, the place where we dwell under your charge is too small for us. 2 Let us go to the **Jordan** and each of us get there a log, and let us make a*

place for us to dwell there." And he answered, "Go." 3 Then one of them said, "Be pleased to go with your servants." And he answered, "I will go." 4 So he went with them. And when they came to the **Jordan**, they cut down trees. 5 But as one was felling a log, his axe head fell into the water, and he cried out, "Alas, my master! It was borrowed." 6 Then the man of God said, "Where did it fall?" When he showed him the place, he cut off a stick and threw it in there and made the iron float. 7 And he said, "Take it up." So he reached out his hand and took it.

8. **John the Baptist baptized many people in the Jordan River.**

    Matthew 3:5–6: *Then Jerusalem and all Judea and all the region about the Jordan were going out to him, 6 and they were baptized by him in the **river Jordan**, confessing their sins.*

9. **Jesus was baptized in the Jordan River by John the Baptist.**

    Matthew 3:13–17: *Then Jesus came from Galilee to the **Jordan** to John, to be baptized by him. 14 John would have prevented him, saying, "I need to be baptized by you, and do you come to me?" 15 But Jesus answered him, "Let it be so now, for thus it is fitting for us to fulfill all righteousness." Then he consented. 16 And when Jesus was baptized, immediately he went up from the water, and*

    Yardenit Baptismal Site

    behold, the heavens were opened to him, and he saw the Spirit of God descending like a dove and coming to rest on him; 17 and behold, a voice from heaven said, "This is my beloved Son, with whom I am well pleased."

10. **The disciples of Jesus baptized many people in the Jordan River.**

    John 4:1–3: *Now when Jesus learned that the Pharisees had heard that Jesus was making and baptizing more disciples than John 2 (although Jesus himself did not baptize, but only his disciples), 3 he left Judea and departed again for Galilee.*

Faith Lesson from the Jordan River

1. The Jordan River represented life and vitality to the Israelites. They were desert people, and water was their life. Therefore, Christ used this concept to teach them that in the same way water was vital for their physical lives, He was vital for their spiritual lives as well. Do we realize the importance of a close relationship with Christ in order to have spiritual life and vitality?

2. The meaning of Jordan means "descend." In a spiritual sense, are we humble before God and submissive to Him in order to grow spiritually?

3. The Israelites crossed the Jordan River on dry ground. In so doing, God reminded them of the miracle of crossing the Red Sea after their exodus from Egypt. Often, God will repeat miracles to show His faithfulness. What things has God done repeatedly to show His faithfulness to us?

Baptismal Site of Jesus

4. Naaman, the leper, had his own idea of how God should operate. Do we often have our own ideas as well as to how we think God should do things?

5. Baptism played a major role in the ministries of John the Baptist, Jesus, and his disciples. It was a baptism of repentance. What is our view of baptism today, and how important is it to us and our ministries?

Journal/Notes:

Jordan River: Baptismal Site of Jesus

Location

There are two main baptismal sites on the Jordan River.

Qasr al-Yahud Baptismal Site

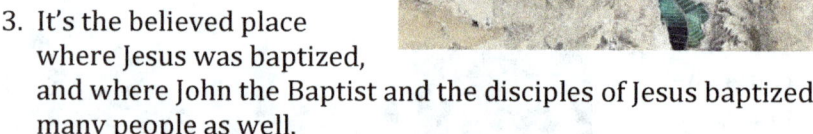

1. It's located about 2 miles (3.2 km.) east of Hwy. 90, across from Jericho.
2. It's also known as Qaser al-Yahud, Kasser al-Yahud, and the Baptismal Site of Jesus.
3. It's the believed place where Jesus was baptized, and where John the Baptist and the disciples of Jesus baptized many people as well.
4. The water is not quite as clean as Yardenit, but thousands of pilgrims are baptized here each year because of its spiritual significance.
5. It's also the believed location where the Israelites crossed the Jordan River to enter the Promised Land.
6. For those desiring to get baptized here in the Jordan River, the Qsar al-Yahud gift shop provides white robes and towels for a small fee.
7. Qsar al-Yahud also has a gift shop for the purchase of souvenirs and other miscellaneous items.

Yardenit Baptismal Site

1. Yardenit is just a couple hundred yards (meters) west of Hwy. 90, at the southern tip of the Sea of Galilee.
2. It's a popular spot, and the water is clean and abundant.
3. For those desiring to get baptized in the Jordan River at Yardenit, their gift shop provides white robes and towels for a small fee.
4. Yardenit has a large gift shop for the purchase of souvenirs and other miscellaneous items as well.

(For more, please see Yardenit Baptismal Site.)

Negev & Southern Israel Sites

Historical Background

1. The concept of baptism is rooted in the Old Testament. As far back as Genesis, eight people were saved from the great flood of God's judgment. The Apostle Peter indicated that the water of the flood "symbolizes baptism that now saves you" (1 Pet. 3:21).

Qasr al-Yahud Baptismal Site – Jordanian sites in background

2. Old Testament prophets such as Isaiah, Ezekiel, and David likewise used water as an external symbol for internal cleansing (Isa. 1:16; Ezek. 36:25; Ps. 51:2).

   Isaiah 1:16: *Wash yourselves; make yourselves clean; remove the evil of your deeds from before my eyes; cease to do evil.*

3. The word baptize, baptized, or baptismal is mentioned around 72 times in the New Testament and, therefore, shows the value God places upon it.

Places of Interest

1. Qasr al-Yahud Baptismal Site
2. Hwy. 90
3. Jew's Palace (Castle of the Jews)
4. Jordanian Baptismal Site of Jesus
5. St. John the Baptist Romanian Church: On the Jordanian Site of the river.
6. Original Church of John the Baptist. There have been at least 5 churches built at this location dating back to the first and second centuries AD.
7. Cave of John the Baptist
8. Greek Orthodox Church of St John the Baptist

9. The believed location where the Israelites crossed the Jordan River to enter the Promised Land.
10. This area is also associated with the ascension of the Prophet Elijah into heaven, which is commemorated at a hill called Tell Mar Elias or Jabal Mar-Elias (Elijah's Hill).

Baptism in the Bible

1. Baptism in the Old Testament.

Baptism in the Old Testament had a different name and purpose than believers' baptism in the New Testament.

- It served as a purification ritual that happened regularly.
- Before entering the temple, a synagogue, or any religious building, the Jews would purify themselves (ritual cleansing) in Mikvahs (purification pools).
- They also purified themselves before the Sabbath, feast days, and so forth. Purification for a Jew was a regular part of life.
- Purification involved confession of sin, entering a pool of water, immersing oneself completely, and putting on a new change of clothes. Mikvahs were found everywhere, and some of the wealthier population had their own private mikvahs.

2. **The Baptism of John the Baptist.**

   John's baptism picked up on this Jewish concept and took it a step further. His baptism was primarily a baptism of repentance in preparation for the coming Messiah.

   Matthew 3:1–6: *In those days John the Baptist came preaching in the wilderness of Judea, 2 "Repent, for the kingdom of heaven is at hand." 3 For this is he who was spoken of by the prophet Isaiah when he said, "The voice of one crying in the wilderness: 'Prepare the way of the Lord; make his paths straight.'" 4 Now John wore a garment of camel's hair and a leather belt around his waist, and his food was locusts and wild honey. 5 Then Jerusalem and all Judea and all the region about the Jordan were going out to him, 6 and they were* **baptized** *by him in the river Jordan,* **confessing their sins**.

3. **Jesus was baptized by John.**

   Matthew 3:13–17: *Then Jesus came from Galilee to the Jordan to John, to be* **baptized** *by him. 14 John would have prevented him, saying, "I need to be* **baptized** *by you, and do you come to me?" 15 But Jesus answered him, "Let it be so now, for thus it is fitting for us to fulfill all righteousness." Then he consented. 16 And when* **Jesus was baptized**, *immediately he went up from the water, and behold, the heavens were opened to him, and he saw the Spirit of God descending like a dove and coming to rest on him; 17 and behold, a voice from heaven said, "This is my beloved Son, with whom I am well pleased."*

   Qasr al-Yahud Baptismal Site

4. **Why did Jesus get baptized if He was God in the flesh and perfect? After all, the purpose of Baptism in Jesus' day was a baptism of repentance.**

   - Jesus permitted John the Baptist to baptize Him in order to fulfill all righteousness.

- He was setting an example for all to follow.
- Jesus didn't repent of anything because He was perfect.
- It also allowed God to speak audibly and show His pleasure and affirmation of Christ as the Son of God.

5. **Jesus' baptism of others.**

   The message and baptism of Jesus dealt with repentance from sin and acceptance of Himself as the Messiah.

   - Matthew 4:17: *From that time Jesus began to preach, saying, "Repent, for the kingdom of heaven is at hand."*
   - John 4:1–3: *Now when Jesus learned that the Pharisees had heard that Jesus was making and* **baptizing** *more disciples than John 2 (although Jesus himself did not baptize, but only his disciples), 3 he left Judea and departed again for Galilee.*

6. **Baptism in the rest of the New Testament.**

   Baptism always followed salvation and was an outward proclamation of an inner conversion.

   - On the day of Pentecost, 3,000 people were saved and were baptized. They would have used the existing Jewish mikvahs as baptismal pools.

     Acts 2:41: *So those who received his word were* **baptized**, *and there were added that day about three thousand souls.*

   - Baptism was an act of obedience symbolizing the believer's faith in a crucified, buried, and risen Savior.

     Romans 6:1–4: *What shall we say then? Are we to continue in sin that grace may abound? 2 By no means! How can we who died to sin still live in it? 3 Do you not know that all of us who have been* **baptized** *into Christ Jesus were* **baptized** *into his death? 4 We were buried therefore with him by* **baptism** *into death, in order*

that, just as Christ was raised from the dead by the glory of the Father, we too might walk in newness of life.

- In the same way Jesus died, was buried, and rose again to new life, baptism follows this same pattern. The believer's placement under the water symbolizes burial and death to sin, and rising up out of the water symbolizes new life in Christ.
- Baptism does not save us in and of itself; it follows salvation and expresses what has already taken place in the heart of a believer.
- Baptism is a declaration to others that we are identifying ourselves with Christ and are now one of His disciples.
- Baptism is commanded in many passages of the Bible, and unless we are unable to do so for some unique reason, we should get baptized.

Matthew 28:18-20: *And Jesus came and said to them, "All authority in heaven and on earth has been given to me. 19 Go therefore and make disciples of all nations, **baptizing them** in the name of the Father and of the Son and of the Holy Spirit, 20 teaching them to observe all that I have commanded you. And behold, I am with you always, to the end of the age."*

Acts 2:37-38: *Now when they heard this they were cut to the heart, and said to Peter and the rest of the apostles, "Brothers, what shall we do?" 38 And Peter said to them, "Repent and be **baptized** every one of you in the name of Jesus Christ for the forgiveness of your sins, and you will receive the gift of the Holy Spirit."*

Faith Lesson on Baptism

1. Jesus didn't need to be baptized but did so in order to be an example for us to follow.
2. If we are genuine believers in Christ and have not been baptized, we should do so in order to obey Christ.
3. Baptism does not save us in and of itself, but when connected with our faith in Christ, it cleanses us of sin, identifies us with the death, burial, and resurrection of Christ, and declares to others that we are followers of Christ.
4. Baptism symbolizes our newness of life in Christ and that we are now dead to being controlled and defeated by sin.

Romans 6:4: *We were buried therefore with him by **baptism** into death, in order that, just as Christ was raised from the dead by the glory of the Father, **we too might walk in newness of life**.*

Journal/Notes:

Jordan River: Crossing into the Promised Land

Location

1. The crossing place where the Israelites entered the Promised Land is just opposite Jericho.
2. It's amazing that it's in the same area where John the Baptist baptized many and where John baptized Jesus.
3. Today, it's known as Qasr el Yahud (Kasser Al Yahud, Qaser), the Baptismal Site of Jesus.
4. It's about 2 miles (3.2 km.) east of Hwy. 90, opposite Jericho.

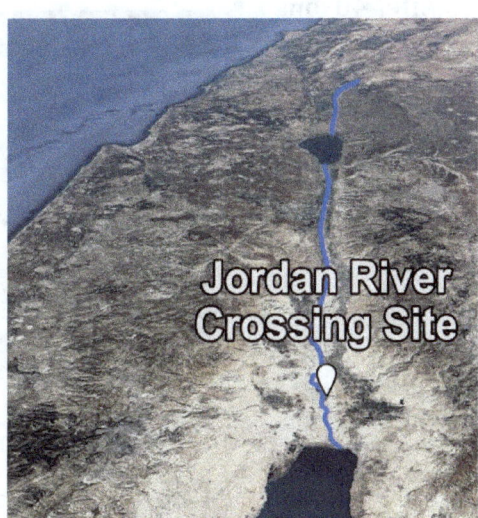

Historical Background

1. The nation of Israel spent 430 years in Egypt. Four hundred of these years, they were slaves (Gen. 15:13), and for 30 years, they enjoyed peace during the time Joseph was alive.
2. God supernaturally delivered the Israelites out of the hands of the Egyptians through Moses.
3. After the Exodus, they crossed the Red Sea on dry ground.
4. They spent a year at Mount Sinai receiving the Law and then headed to Kadesh Barnea to enter the Promised Land.
5. After the 12 spies returned from scouting out the land, 10 spies convinced the people that the inhabitants of the land were too strong for them to conquer, and they should return to Egypt (Num. 13:25–33).
6. Because of their unbelief and disobedience, they were banned from entering the Promised Land and ordered to wander in the desert 40 years until every person 20 years old, and older died (Num. 14:20–25).
7. During the 40 years of wandering in the desert, entering the

Promised Land became a deep yearning within the souls of the new generation. Day after day, they dreamt about a new life in the Promised Land, which would bring an end to their seemingly vain wandering in the desert eating Manna day after day.

8. After 40 long years, they were poised to enter the Promised Land, and their hearts were overflowing with enthusiasm and expectation as the time had finally arrived.

Jordan River crossing location

9. The word "Hebrew" means to cross over. Abraham crossed over from false gods to the one and only true God. He crossed over physically by leaving his homeland and coming to the Promised Land. The Israelites were delivered by God from the Egyptians as they crossed through the Red Sea, and then crossed through the Jordan River into the Promised Land. All these acts are pictures of deliverance and salvation. We also cross over from death to life through Christ.

Places of Interest

1. Crossing Site of the Israelites into the Promised Land.
2. Baptismal Site of Jesus – Believed place where Jesus was baptized and where many are baptized today.
3. Adam – The place where the waters of the Jordan backed up to when the Israelites crossed the river (20 miles, 32 km., above the crossing site).
4. Shittim
5. Camp Gilgal
6. Jericho

Crossing the Jordan River in the Bible

1. **Before entering the Promised Land, the Israelites camped on the east side of the Jordan River, opposite Jericho.**

   Joshua 3:1: *Then Joshua rose early in the morning, and they set out from **Shittim**. And they came to the **Jordan**, he and all the people of Israel, and lodged there before they passed over.*

2. **The Israelites crossed the Jordan River on dry ground as God miraculously parted the waters.**

   Joshua 3:14–17: *So when the people set out from their tents to pass over the **Jordan** with the priests bearing the ark of the covenant before the people, 15 and as soon as those bearing the ark had come as far as the **Jordan**, and the **feet of the priests** bearing the ark were dipped in the brink of the water (**now the Jordan overflows all its banks throughout the time of harvest**), 16 the waters coming down from above stood and rose up in a heap very far away, at **Adam** [20 miles, 32 km. north], the city that is beside Zarethan, and those flowing down toward the Sea of the Arabah, the Salt Sea [Dead Sea], were completely cut off. And the people passed over opposite Jericho. 17 Now the priests bearing the ark of the covenant of the Lord stood firmly on dry ground **in the midst of the Jordan**,* *and all Israel was passing over on dry ground until all the nation finished passing over the **Jordan**.*

Using the geographical layout of the land from Adam to the crossing of the Jordan site, the body of water that would have accumulated would have been 20 miles (32 km.) long, 2 miles (3.2 km.) wide, and around 120 ft. (37 m.) high.

3. **God ordered that 12 stones be taken out of the Jordan River for a monument.**

Joshua 4:1–7: *When all the nation had finished passing over the **Jordan**, the Lord said to Joshua, 2 "Take twelve men from the people, from each tribe a man, 3 and command them, saying, 'Take twelve stones from here out of the midst of the Jordan, from the very place where the priests' feet stood firmly, and bring them over with you and lay them down in the place where you lodge tonight [Gilgal].'" 4 Then Joshua called the twelve men from the people of Israel, whom he had appointed, a man from each tribe. 5 And Joshua said to them, "Pass on before the ark of the Lord your God into the midst of the **Jordan**, and take up each of you a stone upon his shoulder,* *according to the number of the tribes of the people of Israel, 6 that this may be a sign among you. When your children ask in time to come, 'What do those stones mean to you?' 7 then you shall tell them that the waters of the Jordan were cut off before the ark of the covenant of the Lord. When it passed over the **Jordan**, the waters of the **Jordan** were cut off. So these stones shall be to the people of Israel a memorial forever."*

It appears that the 12-Stone Monument was later moved to the permanent Gilgal located about 7 miles north of Camp Gilgal. For more, please see Gilgal.

4. **Joshua also erected a monument in the middle of the Jordan River.**

Jordan River crossing location

Joshua 4:9–10: *And Joshua set up twelve stones in the **midst of the Jordan**, in the place where the feet of the priests bearing the ark of the covenant had stood; and they are there to this day. 10 For the priests bearing the ark stood in the midst of the Jordan until everything was finished that the Lord commanded Joshua to tell the people, according to all that Moses had commanded Joshua.*

5. **After crossing the river, the water flowed again, and the Israelites arrived at Camp Gilgal.**

Joshua 4:15–19: *And the Lord said to Joshua, 16 "Command the priests bearing the ark of the testimony to come up out of the Jordan." 17 So Joshua commanded the priests, "Come up out of the Jordan." 18 And when the priests bearing the ark of the covenant of the Lord came up from the **midst of the Jordan**, and the soles of the priests' feet were lifted up on dry ground, the waters of the Jordan returned to their place and **overflowed all its banks, as before**. 19 The people came up out of the **Jordan** on the tenth day of the first month, and they encamped at **Gilgal** on the east border of Jericho.*

6. Joshua set up 12 stones as a monument of remembrance.

Joshua 4:20–24: *And those twelve stones, which they took out of the **Jordan**, Joshua set up at Gilgal. 21 And he said to the people of Israel, "When your children ask their fathers in times to come, 'What do these stones mean?' 22 then you shall let your children know, 'Israel passed over this Jordan on dry ground.' 23 For the Lord your God dried up the waters of the Jordan for you until you passed over, as the Lord your God **did to the Red Sea**, which he dried up for us until we passed over, 24 so that all the peoples of the earth may know that the hand of the Lord is mighty, that you may fear the Lord your God forever."*

Jordan River crossing location

Faith Lesson from Crossing the Jordan River

1. Entering the Promised Land was a long-awaited dream for the new generation of Israelites after wandering in the desert for 40 years. It was also the fulfillment of the Abrahamic Covenant of promise, one of the foundational covenants in the Bible. Is there some hope and dream you have that seems like it will never happen? Do you also really believe that God will fulfill His promise of heaven and that one day you'll actually be there? And are you living in such a way that shows this?

2. Crossing into the Promised Land is also a picture of living in victory. Unfortunately, many Christians today choose to live in the wilderness in defeat and disobedience. Are you living in obedience and victory or living in the wilderness?

3. The crossing of the Jordan was a much bigger miracle than we think as the river was at flood stage, overflowing its banks. As mentioned, the body of water that would have accumulated would

have been 20 miles (32 km.) long, 2 miles (3.2 km.) wide, and around 120 ft. (37 m.) high. This was a massive body and wall of water the 3 million or more Israelites would have witnessed as they walked alongside it for about 2 miles (3.2 km.).

4. The miracle was similar to the crossing of the Red Sea after the Israelite's Exodus from Egypt. God repeated this miracle to reveal His glory and faithfulness.

5. The waters of the Jordan stopped flowing the moment the priests' stepped into the water. God required the priests to take a step of faith, and then He acted. In the same way, God often asks us to take a step of faith before He moves. What step of faith do we need to take in our lives today?

Jordan River crossing location

6. God ordered Joshua to set up a memorial after crossing the Jordan. Do we have memorials in our minds as reminders of the miracles God has done for us, and do we pass these memorials on to our offspring?

Journal/Notes:

Judean Wilderness

Location

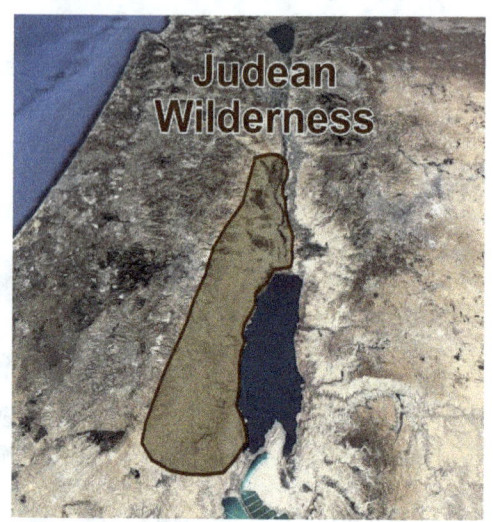

1. The Judean Wilderness runs from north of Jericho to the southern end of the Dead Sea.
2. It lies on the western side of the lower Jordan Valley and the Dead Sea area.
3. It's about 60 miles (95 km.) long and about 13 miles (21 km.) wide.
4. It receives less than 2 inches (50 mm.) of rain per year.
5. Average high temperatures in the winter run in the 70s (21 C.), and highs in the summer run over 100 (40 C.).
6. Water is scarce and hard to find, and very little vegetation grows in the wilderness due to its lack of water and poor soil composition.

Historical Background

1. Even though the Judean Desert is dry and barren, it was settled long before recorded history began. Jericho, which dates to 5000 BC, is the oldest city in the Judean Desert and the oldest continually inhabited city in the world.
2. En Gedi is another notable place that dates to about the same time as Jericho. It's a large oasis that had cities built around it for over 5,000 years.
3. Sodom, Gomorrah, and the other three cities around the Dead Sea date back to ancient times as well.
4. It appears God changed the climate of the Judean Wilderness after He destroyed Sodom and Gomorrah and the surrounding cities. Scripture says that this area used to be like a watered garden of the Lord.

   Genesis 13:10: *And Lot lifted up his eyes and saw that the Jordan*

Negev & Southern Israel Sites

*Valley was **well watered everywhere like the garden of the Lord**, like the land of Egypt, in the direction of Zoar. (This was before the **Lord destroyed Sodom and Gomorrah**.)*

5. God will cause the Judean Wilderness to flourish again during the Millennial Reign of Christ on this earth.

   Ezekiel 47:6–10: *Then he led me back to the bank of the river. 7 As I went back, I saw on the bank of the river very many trees on the one side and on the other. 8 And he said to me, "This water flows toward the eastern region and goes down into the Arabah, and enters the sea; when the water flows into the sea, the water will become fresh. 9 And wherever the river goes, every living creature that swarms will live, and there will be very many fish. For this water goes there, that the waters of the sea may become fresh; so everything will live where the river goes. 10 Fishermen will stand beside the sea. From **En Gedi to Eneglaim** it will be a place for the spreading of nets."*

Places of Interest

1. Judean Wilderness
2. Jordan River

3. Jericho
4. Qumran
5. Dead Sea
6. En Gedi
7. Masada

Judean Wilderness in the Bible

En Gedi and King David

1. **En Gedi was one of David's main hideouts when Saul was pursuing his life.**

   1 Samuel 23:28-29: *So Saul returned from pursuing after David and went against the Philistines. Therefore, that place was called the Rock of Escape. 29 And David went up from there and lived in the* ***strongholds of En Gedi***.

Qumran and the Essenes

1. The Essenes lived in the Judean Wilderness from about 200 BC to around 68 AD. They were a spiritually devoted group who left Jerusalem due to their belief that the priesthood had become corrupt. They devoted themselves to the study and strict obedience of Scripture.

Qumran

2. They also devoted themselves to copying and translating the Bible. When they saw the nation of Israel falling to the Romans in 68 AD, they hid their translations in caves by the Dead Sea.
3. These translated manuscripts are called the Dead Sea Scrolls and were discovered in eleven caves along the northwest shore of the Dead Sea between the years 1947 and 1956.

John the Baptist

1. **He was the prophesied forerunner of Christ, whose purpose was to prepare the way of the Lord (Isa. 40:3).**

2. His main message was a message of repentance.

Matthew 3:1–12: *In those days John the Baptist came preaching in the **wilderness of Judea**, 2 "Repent, for the kingdom of heaven is at hand." 3 For this is he who was spoken of by the prophet Isaiah when he said, "The voice of one **crying in the wilderness**: 'Prepare the way of the Lord; make his paths straight.'" 4 Now John wore a garment of camel's hair and a leather belt around his waist [similar to Elijah], and his food was locusts and wild honey. 5 Then Jerusalem and all Judea and all the region about the Jordan were going out to him, 6 and they were baptized by him in the river Jordan, confessing their sins. 7 But when he saw many of the Pharisees and Sadducees coming to his baptism, he said to them, "You brood of vipers! Who warned you to flee from the wrath to come? 8 Bear fruit in keeping with repentance. 9 And do not presume to say to yourselves, 'We have Abraham as our father,' for I tell you, God is able from these stones to raise up children for Abraham. 10 Even now the axe is laid to the root of the trees. Every tree, therefore, that does not bear good fruit is cut down and thrown into the fire. 11 I baptize you with water for repentance, but he who is coming after me is mightier than I, whose sandals I am not worthy to carry. He will baptize you with the Holy Spirit and fire. 12 His winnowing fork is in his hand, and he will clear his threshing floor and gather his wheat into the barn, but the chaff he will burn with unquenchable fire."*

Judean Wilderness

3. He had the privilege of baptizing Jesus.

Matthew 3:13–17: *Then Jesus came from Galilee to the Jordan to John, to be **baptized by him**. 14 John would have prevented him, saying, "I need to be baptized by you, and do you come to me?" 15 But Jesus answered him, "Let it be so now, for thus it is fitting for us to fulfill all righteousness." Then he consented. 16 And when Jesus was baptized, immediately he went up from the water, 17 and behold, the heavens were opened to him, and he saw the Spirit of God descending like a dove and coming to rest on him; and behold, a* voice from heaven said, "This is my beloved Son, with whom I am well pleased."

4. He was beheaded for taking a stand against sin.

Herod Antipas became the ruler (tetrarch) of Galilee and Perea from 4 BC to 39 AD. He ruled from his capital at Tiberias on the western shore of the Sea of Galilee. He divorced his first wife in order to marry Herodias, the wife of his half-brother Herod Philip. He imprisoned and beheaded John the Baptist for criticizing his marriage (Matt. 14:1–12).

Testing of Jesus

1. After Jesus was baptized, He was immediately led into the wilderness to be tested.

Matthew 4:1–11: *Then Jesus was led up by the Spirit **into the wilderness** to be tempted [tested] by the devil. 2 And after fasting forty days and forty nights, he was hungry. 3 And the tempter came and said to him, "If you are the Son of God, command these stones to become loaves of bread." 4 But he answered, "It is written,*

Judean Wilderness

"'Man shall not live by bread alone, but by every word that comes from the mouth of God.'" 5 Then the devil took him to the holy city and set him on the pinnacle of the temple 6 and said to him, "If you are the Son of God, throw yourself down, for it is written, "'He will command his angels concerning you,' and "'On their hands they will bear you up, lest you strike your foot against a stone.'" 7 Jesus said to him, "Again it is written, 'You shall not put the Lord your God to the test.'" 8 Again, the devil took him to a very high mountain and showed him all the kingdoms of the world and their glory. 9 And he said to him, "All these I will give you, if you will fall down and worship me." 10 Then Jesus said to him, "Be gone, Satan! For it is written, "'You shall worship the Lord your God and him only shall you serve.'" 11 Then the devil left him, and behold, angels came and were ministering to him.

Faith Lesson from the Judean Wilderness

1. John the Baptist was a strong and serious witness for Jesus. John's life is an example to us of the seriousness with which we are to approach the Christian life and our call to ministry.

Judean Wilderness, Dead Sea

2. John shows us how to stand firm in our faith no matter what the circumstances. Paul reminds us that "everyone who wants to live a godly life in Christ Jesus will be persecuted" (2 Tim. 3:12).
3. Christ was tested and overcame each test of Satan with Scripture.
4. God tested many of His servants before He called them to ministry, i.e., Moses, David, and the prophets.
5. We are often tested by God as well.
6. Scripture says that leaders are to be tested before being placed into ministry (1 Tim. 3:10).
7. Has God tested me in various ways in my lifetime?
8. How have I responded to the tests He sends my way?
9. Do I know God's Word so I can overcome the temptations of Satan?

Journal/Notes:

Kadesh Barnea

Location

1. Kadesh Barnea is on the southern border area between Israel and Egypt.
2. It's about 31 miles (51 km.) east of the Mediterranean Ocean and about 33 miles (53 km.) southwest of Beer Sheba.
3. Kadesh Barnea was the original place where God intended the Israelites to enter the Promised Land.
4. Today, a community lives at Kadesh Barnea, and the town retains its same name.

Historical Background

1. At Kadesh Barnea, one of the most tragic events in Israel's history happened.
2. It's here they rebelled against God's plan for them to enter the Promised Land. As a result, they were severely judged for their lack of faith and condemned to wander in the wilderness 40 years until those 20 years old, and older died.
3. The Israelites had seen many spectacular miracles.
   - They saw 10 supernatural plagues God sent upon the Egyptians.
   - They witnessed the first Passover wherein God spared the Israelites as they put blood from a lamb around the doors of their dwellings.
   - They saw God open the hearts of the Egyptians so that they gave them many possessions.
   - They experienced supernatural help to cross the Sinai Peninsula on eagle's wings to reach the Aqaba finger of the Red Sea.

Negev & Southern Israel Sites

- They beheld a pillar of cloud by day and a pillar of fire by night to guide and protect them.
- They experienced the miraculous crossing of the Red Sea (10.5 miles wide, 17 km.) in which they were approximately 2,500 ft. (762 m.) under sea level in the midst of the depths and mighty waters of the sea (Isa. 51:10).
- They saw God supernaturally provide water out of a rock at Rephidim.
- God helped the Israelites supernaturally defeat the Amalekites as Aaron and Hur held up the arms of Moses.
- They stood in fear and trembling as God sent fire and smoke upon Mt. Sinai when he gave them the Ten Commandments written on stone by His own finger.

Modern-day Kadesh Barnea

- They received supernatural provisions of Manna and quail in the desert.
4. The Israelites had been bathed in miracles for well over a year from when they left Egypt until they reached Kadesh Barnea.
5. They had seen enough miracles to be able to trust God for anything.
6. However, despite all the miracles they had witnessed, they viewed God as too weak to help them enter the Promised Land and rebelled against Him.

Places of Interest

1. Kadesh Barnea
2. Egypt
3. Sinai Peninsula
4. Aqaba Finger of the Red Sea Crossing
5. Rephidim

6. Mt. Sinai
7. Israel

Kadesh Barnea in the Bible

1. **Twelve spies were sent into the Promised Land from Kadesh Barnea to give a report.**

    Numbers 13:1–3: *Then the Lord spoke to Moses saying, 2 "Send out for yourself men so that they may spy out the **land of Canaan**, which I am going to **give to the sons of Israel**; you shall send a man from each of their fathers' tribes, every one a leader among them." 3 So Moses sent them from the wilderness of Paran at the command of the Lord, all of them men who were heads of the sons of Israel.*

2. **Ten Spies give a bad report of the difficulty in possessing the land.**

    Numbers 13:25–29: *When they returned from **spying out the land**, at the end of forty days, 26 they proceeded to come to Moses and Aaron and to all the congregation of the sons of Israel in the wilderness of Paran, at **Kadesh**; and they brought back word to them and to all the congregation and showed them the fruit of the* land. 27 Thus, they told him, and said, "We went in to the land where you sent us; and it certainly does flow with milk and honey, and this is its fruit. 28 Nevertheless, the people who live in the land are strong, and the cities are fortified and very large; and moreover, we saw the descendants of Anak there. 29 Amalek is living in the land of the Negev and the Hittites and the Jebusites and the Amorites are living in the hill country, and the Canaanites are living by the sea and by the side of the Jordan."

3. **Two spies (Joshua and Caleb) give a good report of faith. Caleb is the spokesman.**

    Numbers 13:30: *Then Caleb quieted the people before Moses and said, "We should by all means go up and take possession of it, for we will surely overcome it."*

4. **The 10 spies convince the people that they are unable to possess the land.**

    Numbers 13:31–33: *But the men who had gone up with him said, "We are **not able to go up against the people**, for they are **too strong for us**." 32 So they gave out to the sons of Israel a bad report of the land which they had spied out, saying, "The land through which we have gone, in spying it out, is a land that devours its inhabitants; and all the people whom we saw in it are men of great size. 33 There also we saw the Nephilim (the sons of Anak are part of the Nephilim); and we became like grasshoppers in our own sight, and so we were in their sight."*

    Modern-day Kadesh Barnea

5. **The Israelites rebel against God and decide to return to Egypt as slaves again.**

    Numbers 14:1–4: *Then all the congregation lifted up their voices and cried, and the people wept that night. 2 All the sons of Israel grumbled against Moses and Aaron; and the whole congregation said to them, "Would that we had died in the land of Egypt! Or would that we had died in this wilderness! 3 Why is the Lord bringing us* into this land, to fall by the sword? Our wives and our little ones will become plunder; would it not be better for us to return to Egypt?" 4 So they said to one another, "**Let us appoint a leader and return to Egypt.**"

6. **Moses, Aaron, Joshua, and Caleb plead with the people not to rebel against God's will for them.**

    Numbers 14:5–10: *Then Moses and Aaron fell on their faces in the presence of all the assembly of the congregation of the sons of Israel. 6 Joshua the son of Nun and Caleb the son of Jephunneh, of those who had spied out the land, tore their clothes; 7 and they spoke to all the congregation of the sons of Israel, saying, "The land which we passed through to spy out is an exceedingly good land. 8 If the Lord is pleased with us, then He will bring us into this land and give it to us— a land which flows with milk and honey. 9 Only do not rebel against*

    Kadesh Barnea countryside

    the Lord; and do not fear the people of the land, for they will be our prey. Their protection has been removed from them, and the Lord is with us; do not fear them." 10 But all the congregation said to stone them with stones. Then the glory of the Lord appeared in the tent of meeting to all the sons of Israel.

7. **God threatens to destroy the Israelites and make a great nation out of Moses' offspring.**

    Numbers 14:11–12: *The Lord said to Moses, "How long will this people spurn Me? And how long will they not believe in Me, despite all the signs which I have performed in their midst? 12 I will smite them with pestilence and dispossess them, and I will make you into a nation greater and mightier than they."*

8. **Moses prays on behalf of the people (Num. 14:13–19).**

9. **God forgives the Israelites but still judges them.**

    Numbers 14:20–38: *So the Lord said, "**I have pardoned them according to your word**; 21 but indeed, as I live, all the earth will be filled with the glory of the Lord. 22 Surely all the men who have* *seen My glory and My signs which I performed in Egypt and in the wilderness, yet have put Me to the test these ten times and have not listened to My voice, 23* **shall by no means see the land which I swore to their fathers***, nor shall any of those who spurned Me see it. 24 But My servant Caleb, because he has had a different spirit and has followed Me fully, I will bring into the land which he entered, and his descendants shall take possession of it. 25 Now the Amalekites and the Canaanites live in the valleys; turn tomorrow and set out to the wilderness by the way of the Red Sea."*

26 The Lord spoke to Moses and Aaron, saying, 27 "How long shall I bear with this evil congregation who are grumbling against Me? I have heard the complaints of the sons of Israel, which they are making against Me. 28 Say to them, 'As I live,' says the Lord, 'just as you have spoken in My hearing, so I will surely do to you; 29 your corpses will fall in this wilderness, even all your numbered men,

Kadesh Barnea countryside

according to your complete number from twenty years old and upward, who have grumbled against Me. 30 Surely you shall not come into the land in which I swore to settle you, except Caleb the son of Jephunneh and Joshua the son of Nun. 31 Your children, however, whom you said would become a prey—I will bring them in, and they will know the land which you have rejected. 32 But as for you, your corpses will fall in this wilderness. 33 Your sons shall be shepherds for forty years in the wilderness, and they will suffer for your unfaithfulness, until your corpses lie in the wilderness. 34 According to the number of days which you spied out the land, forty days, for every day you shall bear your guilt a year, even forty years, and you will know My opposition. 35 I, the Lord, have spoken, surely this I will do to all this evil congregation who are gathered together against Me. In this wilderness they shall be destroyed, and there they will die.'" 36 As for the men whom Moses sent to spy out the land and who returned and made all the congregation grumble against him by bringing out a bad report concerning the land, 37 even those men who brought out the very bad report of the land died by a plague before the Lord. 38 But Joshua the son of Nun and Caleb the son of Jephunneh remained alive out of those men who went to spy out the land.

Faith Lesson from Kadesh Barnea

1. The reality of the judgment of God is sobering. God forgave the Israelites, but He did not remove the consequences of their disobedience. We frequently find this in Scripture, i.e., Moses striking the rock and David and his sin with Bathsheba.
2. There were approximately 1.2 million Israelites 20 years old and above who died in the desert over a 40-year period. This means there were 30,000 funerals per year, 82 funerals a day, and 7 funerals an hour.
3. God has written these examples in the Bible for our instruction today.

   Romans 15:4: *For whatever **was written in earlier times was written for our instruction**, so that through perseverance and the encouragement of the Scriptures we might have hope.*

   Modern-day Kadesh Barnea

   1 Corinthians 10:1–13: *For I do not want you to be unaware, brethren, that our fathers were all under the cloud and all passed through the sea; 2 and all were baptized into Moses in the cloud and in the sea; 3 and all ate the same spiritual food; 4 and all drank the same spiritual drink, for they were drinking from a spiritual rock which followed them; and the rock was Christ. 5 Nevertheless, with most of them God was not well-pleased; for they were laid low in the wilderness. 6 Now these things happened as examples for us, so that we would not crave evil things as they also craved. 7 Do not be idolaters, as some of them were; as it is written, "The people sat*

down to eat and drink, and stood up to play." 8 Nor let us act immorally, as some of them did, and twenty-three thousand fell in one day. 9 Nor let us try the Lord, as some of them did, and were destroyed by the serpents. 10 Nor grumble, as some of them did, and were destroyed by the destroyer. 11 **Now these things happened to them as an example, and they were written for our instruction**, upon whom the ends of the ages have come. 12 Therefore, let him who thinks he stands take heed that he does not fall. 13 No temptation has overtaken you but such as is common to man; and God is faithful, who will not allow you to be tempted beyond what you are able, but with the temptation will provide the way of escape also, so that you will be able to endure it.

Wilderness of Paran by Kadesh Barnea

4. Do I grumble and complain about God's provisions, trials, or difficulties He has sent my way?
5. Do I have faith that God can help me in whatever He has called me to do and be?

Journal/Notes:

Lachish

Location

1. Tel Lachish is in the foothills (Shaphelah) of the Judean Mountains, about 18 miles (30 km.) from the Mediterranean Sea and about 25 miles (41 km.) southwest of Jerusalem.
2. Lachish is regarded as the second most important city after Jerusalem in the Southern Kingdom of Judah and was strategically located on the Via Maris travel route.
3. It was a well-fortified military city with double walls and provided protection to Israel's southern region.

Historical Background

1. Lachish has two major settlement periods, a Canaanite and an Israelite settlement period.
2. Lachish was first settled and inhabited by the Canaanites around 3000 BC.
3. It was then conquered by the Israelites under Joshua during the conquest of the Promised Land.
4. After the Kingdom of Israel was divided, Lachish became a thriving Israelite city during king Rehoboam's reign (920 BC), and around 10,000 people lived in the city at that time.
5. It was destroyed by the Assyrians in 701 BC and by the Babylonians in 587 BC.
6. Numerous pottery shards (ostraca) were found at Lachish. One spoke of the fall of the nearby city of Azekah (above the Valley of Elah) by the Assyrians. This realization must have sent fear into the hearts of those in Lachish. Another pottery shard spoke of a prophet, most likely Jeremiah.

7. Writings and relief pictures at Nineveh (modern-day Mosul) reveal the destruction of Lachish.
8. Interestingly, ostraca pieces and other findings in Israel reveal the evidence of around 100 biblical names of people in the Bible.
9. There are 2 caves filled with skulls nearby to Lachish, giving evidence of its destruction.
10. In 539 BC, the Persians defeated the Babylonians and allowed the exiles to return to Israel from 538–445 BC. Jerusalem and Lachish were reconstructed at this time (Nehemiah 11:1, 30).
11. Lachish was finally abandoned after the Hellenistic rule in Israel (332–167 BC).

Places of Interest

1. Entrance
2. Large Building
3. Siege Ramp
4. City Gate
5. Palace
6. Palace Courtyard

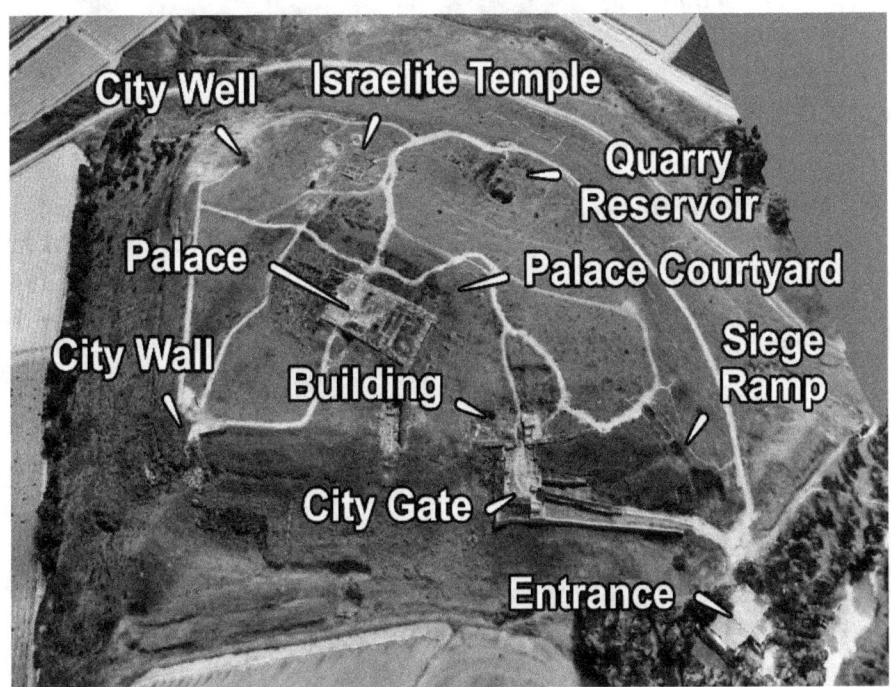

7. Quarry/Reservoir
8. Israelite Temple – Similar layout as the temple in Tel Arad. This temple was also prohibited (Deut. 12:5–7).
9. City Well
10. City Walls

Lachish in the Bible

1. **The King of Lachish joined 4 other kings to fight against the Gibeonites because they had made peace with Israel during the conquest of the Promised Land.**

   Joshua 10:1–5: *As soon as Adoni-zedek, king of Jerusalem, heard how Joshua had captured Ai and had devoted it to destruction, doing to Ai and its king as he had done to Jericho and its king, and how the inhabitants of Gibeon had made peace with Israel and were among them, 2 he feared greatly, because Gibeon was a great city,*

   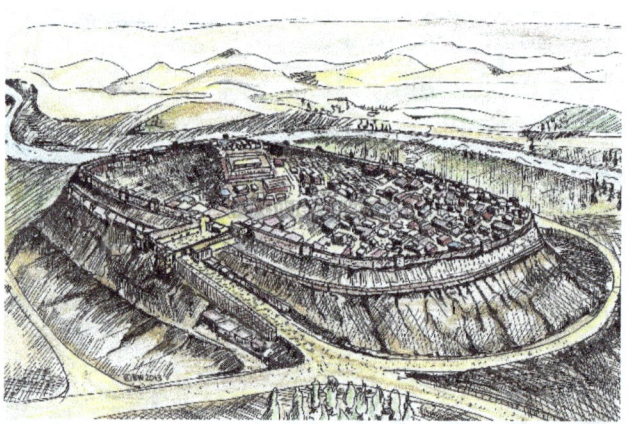
   Lachish replica

   *like one of the royal cities, and because it was greater than Ai, and all its men were warriors. 3 So Adoni-zedek king of Jerusalem sent to Hoham king of Hebron, to Piram king of Jarmuth, to **Japhia king of Lachish**, and to Debir king of Eglon, saying, 4 "Come up to me and help me, and let us strike Gibeon. For it has made peace with Joshua and with the people of Israel." 5 Then the five kings of the Amorites, the king of Jerusalem, the king of Hebron, the king of Jarmuth, the **king of Lachish**, and the king of Eglon, gathered their forces and went up with all their armies and encamped against Gibeon and made war against it.*

2. **Joshua prayed that the sun would stand still so the Israelites could defeat the 5 kings who had gathered to make war against the Gibeonites and the Israelites.**

   Joshua 10:10–14: *And the Lord threw them into a panic before*

Israel, who struck them with a great blow at Gibeon and chased them by the way of the ascent of Beth-horon and struck them as far as Azekah and Makkedah. 11 And as they fled before Israel, while they were going down the ascent of Beth-horon, the Lord threw down **large stones** from heaven on them as far as Azekah, and they died. There were more who died because of the hailstones than the sons of Israel killed with the sword. 12 At that time Joshua spoke to the Lord in the day when the Lord gave the Amorites over to the sons of Israel, and he said in the sight of Israel, "**Sun, stand still** at Gibeon, and moon, in the Valley of Aijalon." 13 And the **sun stood still, and the moon stopped**, until the nation took vengeance on their enemies. Is this not written in the Book of Jashar? The sun stopped in the midst of heaven and did not hurry to set for about a whole day. 14 There has been no day like it before or since, when the Lord heeded the voice of a man, for the Lord fought for Israel.

City Gate

3. **Joshua and the Israelites conquer Lachish.**

    Joshua 10:31–32: *Then Joshua and all Israel with him passed on from Libnah to **Lachish** and laid siege to it and fought against it. 32 And the Lord gave **Lachish** into the hand of Israel, and he captured it on the second day and struck it with the edge of the sword, and every person in it, as he had done to Libnah.*

4. **King Rehoboam, Solomon's son, fortified Lachish in about 920 BC after the kingdom of Israel was divided.**

    2 Chronicles 11:5–12: *Rehoboam lived in Jerusalem, and he built cities for defense in Judah. 6 He built Bethlehem, Etam, Tekoa, 7 Beth-zur, Soco, Adullam, 8 Gath, Mareshah, Ziph, 9 Adoraim, **Lachish**, Azekah, 10 Zorah, Aijalon, and Hebron, fortified cities that are in Judah and in Benjamin. 11 He made the **fortresses strong**, and put commanders in them, and stores of food, oil, and wine. 12*

And he put shields and spears in all the cities and made them very strong. So he held Judah and Benjamin.

5. **King Amaziah fled to Lachish after his defeat to the Northern Kingdom of Israel and was killed by his own countrymen in 767 BC.**

   2 Chronicles 25:14–15: *After Amaziah came from striking down the Edomites, he brought the gods of the men of Seir and set them up as his gods and worshiped them, making offerings to them. 15 Therefore the Lord was angry with Amaziah and sent to him a prophet, who said to him, "Why have you sought the gods of a people who did not deliver their own people from your hand?"*

   Siege Ramp at Lachish

   2 Chronicles 25:27: *From the time when he [Amaziah] turned away from the Lord, they made a conspiracy against him in Jerusalem, and he fled to **Lachish**. But they sent after him to **Lachish** and put him to death there.*

6. **God destroyed Lachish because of their continual rejection of Him and sinful choices.**

   Micah 1:13: *Harness the steeds to the chariots, inhabitants of **Lachish**; it was the beginning of sin to the daughter of Zion, for in you were found the transgressions of Israel.*

7. **Lachish was attacked and destroyed by the Assyrians in 701 BC.**

   After Assyria conquered the Northern Kingdom of Israel and led them into captivity to Assyria in 722 BC, King Sennacherib set his sights on Egypt and Judah in 701 BC.

   2 Kings 18:13: *In the fourteenth year of King Hezekiah, Sennacherib king of Assyria came up against **all the fortified cities of Judah** and took them.*

   2 Chronicles 32:9–10: *After this, Sennacherib king of Assyria, who*

was besieging **Lachish** *with all his forces, sent his servants to Jerusalem to Hezekiah king of Judah and to all the people of Judah who were in Jerusalem, saying, 10 "Thus says Sennacherib king of Assyria, 'On what are you trusting, that you endure the siege in Jerusalem?'"*

In the destruction of Lachish, as many as 50,000 people were tortured and killed when Sennacherib took it. Based on archaeological discoveries and writings in Nineveh, the Assyrians beheaded, burned, flayed, and impaled those they conquered.

Those who escaped death were deported to Assyria, led by rings pierced through their lips.

In the writings of Sennacherib, he mentions how his army penetrated fortifications using ramps,

Palace and Courtyard

battering rams, mines, breeches, and siege engines. The evidence of these tactics can be seen in the siege ramp at Lachish.

8. God supernaturally protected Jerusalem from the Assyrian conquest.

After King Sennacherib conquered Lachish and the southern cities of Judah, he set his sights on Jerusalem. The deliverance of Jerusalem in 701 BC, under King Hezekiah's godly leadership, is one of the most pivotal and monumental miracles in Israel's history. Assyria rose to world domination and had conquered all the Northern Kingdom of Israel and all the southern cities of Judah. Jerusalem was the only city left in the whole region that had not fallen. Assyria was hungry and ready to devour Jerusalem by its merciless iron-toothed war machine.

2 Kings 19:8–10: *The Rabshakeh returned, and found the king of Assyria fighting against Libnah, for he heard that the king had left* **Lachish**. *9 Now the king heard concerning Tirhakah king of Cush, "Behold, he has set out to fight against you." So he sent messengers*

again to Hezekiah, saying, 10 "Thus shall you speak to Hezekiah king of Judah: 'Do not let your God in whom you trust deceive you by promising that Jerusalem will not be given into the hand of the king of Assyria.'"

2 Kings 19:20: *Then Isaiah the son of Amoz sent to Hezekiah, saying, "Thus says the Lord, the God of Israel:* **Your prayer** *to me about Sennacherib king of Assyria I have heard."*

2 Kings 19:35–37: *And that night the angel of the Lord went out and* **struck down 185,000** *in the camp of the Assyrians. And when people arose early in the morning, behold, these were all dead bodies. 36 Then Sennacherib king of Assyria departed and went home and lived at Nineveh. 37 And as he was worshiping in the house of Nisroch his god, Adrammelech and Sharezer, his sons, struck him down with the sword and escaped into the land of Ararat. And Esarhaddon his son reigned in his place.*

Tel Lachish aerial view

The defeat over Sennacherib at Jerusalem was a devastating blow to the Assyrian Empire, which caused it to spiral downward thereafter. Later, the Babylonian Empire would arise and become the new world power.

9. **Lachish was again destroyed by the Babylonians in around 587 BC.**

   Jeremiah 34:6–7: *Then Jeremiah the prophet spoke all these words to Zedekiah king of Judah, in Jerusalem, 7 when the army of the king of Babylon was fighting against Jerusalem and against all the cities of Judah that were left,* **Lachish** *and Azekah, for these were the only fortified cities of Judah that remained.*

10. **The destruction and deportations of the Israelites into Assyria and Babylon were because of their continual disobedience to God.**

    Ezra 5:12: *But because our fathers had provoked the God of heaven to wrath, He gave them into the hand of Nebuchadnezzar king of Babylon, the Chaldean, who destroyed this temple and deported the people to Babylon.*

Ezra 9:7: *Since the days of our fathers to this day we have been in great guilt, and on account of our iniquities we, our kings and our priests have been given into the hand of the kings of the lands, to the sword, to captivity and to plunder and to open shame, as it is this day.*

Faith Lesson from Lachish

1. God gave the Israelites a great victory over the king of Lachish by causing the sun to stand still and sending great hailstones. Joshua demonstrated great faith in asking God to cause the sun to stand still. Do we realize God is able to do great miracles in our lives if we have faith like Joshua?

2. God supernaturally protected Jerusalem because of King Hezekiah's devotion and faith and defeated the Assyrians by ordering one angel to kill 185,000 soldiers. If our hearts are right before God, there is nothing we should fear.

Tel Lachish entry

3. However, around 115 years later, God allowed the Israelites to be conquered by the Babylonians because of their continual sinful choices. When we are not right with God, we find ourselves in the hand of a disciplining God who will deal with us according to His wisdom.

Journal/Notes:

Masada

Location

1. Masada is at the southern end of the Dead Sea, about 40 miles (64 km.) southeast of Jerusalem.
2. It's a natural flat mountain that rises up from the valley floor some 1,000 ft. (305 m.). It's like a huge column with sheer cliffs on every side that makes it virtually unreachable.
3. Ancient Gomorrah lies at the base of Masada, and ancient Sodom is south of Masada, about 14 miles (23 km.).

4. The base of Masada is in a desert region about 1,000 ft. (305 m.) below sea level.
5. The word Masada means fortress.

Historical Background Leading up to the Fall of Masada

1. Masada was one of 3 fortified fortresses King Herod built for pleasure purposes and from which to protect his territories. He built Masada in about 24 BC.
2. Masada was fortified with elaborate water cisterns that were fed by diverting water from the nearby mountains. It even had swimming pools and most of the luxuries life afforded at that time.
3. In addition to ample water storage, Masada had 15 storehouses of food, enough for 10,000 people for 10 years.
4. In 66 AD, events began to unfold in Israel that caused the Jews to rebel against Roman rule. This revolt began in Caesarea Maritime.
5. In 66–70 AD, when the nation was in revolt, Jewish Zealots who had fled from Jerusalem and the surrounding areas took the fortress of Masada from Roman occupation. They were national Freedom Fighters who opposed Roman rule. In their conquest, they gained possession of all the stored food and water at Masada.

Negev & Southern Israel Sites

6. Between 66–70 AD, Rome conquered all the northern cities of Israel.
7. In 70 AD, under the command of Titus, the Romans totally destroyed Jerusalem in a bloody battle that lasted well over 4 months. Josephus (Jewish Historian) claims that 1.1 million Jews lost their lives in this battle, and another 97,000 were captured and enslaved. The temple was leveled in the siege at this time as well.
8. In 73 AD, there had amassed a total of 967 Jews, counting their families, at Masada. They were under the command of Eleazar Ben-Yair, a Jewish Zealot Freedom Fighter.
9. After conquering Jerusalem and most of Israel, the Romans headed south to conquer the southern strongholds around the Dead Sea region and Masada.

Masada view from the north

10. Masada was the last stronghold of the Israelites that existed, and the Romans amassed their troops there in the fall of 73 AD.

Places of Interest

1. Cistern
2. Living Quarters
3. Ritual Baths
4. Small Palace 1
5. Southern Fort
6. Pool
7. Small Palace 2
8. Small Palace 3
9. Western Palace
10. Byzantine Church

11. Cable Car Access

12. Eastern Gate
13. Storerooms
14. Baths
15. Northern Palace
16. Officers' Quarters
17. Administrative Building
18. Western Gate
19. Synagogue
20. Siege Ramp
21. En Gedi
22. Dead Sea
23. Ancient Gomorrah
24. Ancient Sodom

Masada in the Bible

1. **After a confrontation between King Saul and David close to En Gedi, David likely hid out on top of Masada afterward.**

    1 Samuel 24:22: *And David swore this to Saul. Then Saul went home, but David and his men went up to the **stronghold [fortress]**.*

2. **Because of Israel's rejection of Christ as their Messiah, Christ foretold the destruction of Jerusalem and the nation of Israel. This destruction occurred between 66–74 AD.**

    Luke 19:41–44: *And when he drew near and saw the city, he wept over it, 42 saying, "Would that you, even you, had known on this day the things that make for peace! But now they are hidden from your eyes. 43 For the days will come upon you, when your enemies will set up a barricade around you and surround you and hem you in on every side 44 and tear you down to the ground, you and your children within you. And they will not leave one stone upon another in you, because you did not know the time of your visitation."*

3. **Zechariah prophesied about Jerusalem's destruction as well.**

   Zechariah 14:1-2: *Behold, a day is coming for the Lord, when the spoil taken from you will be divided in your midst. 2 For I will gather all the nations against Jerusalem to battle, and the city shall be taken and the houses plundered and the women raped. Half of the city shall go out into exile, but the rest of the people shall not be cut off from the city.*

The Fall of Masada

1. In 73 AD, the 10th Roman Army Legion, totaling around 10,000 soldiers and 6,000 Jewish slaves under a commander by the name of Silva, arrived at the base of Masada.
2. This Roman legion first built a wall around the base of Masada, much of it by using Jewish slave labor.
3. Next, they built 8 camps around the base of the mountain. The remains of most of these camps can still be seen today. Silva set up his headquarters at the northwest camp.
4. After several months of unsuccessful engagement with the Jewish Zealots atop Masada, the Romans decided to build a massive siege ramp out of dirt on the west side of Masada using Israelite slave labor to help in the process.
5. As the siege ramp grew closer to the top of Masada, the Romans primarily used Jewish slave labor so that their fellow Jews on Masada wouldn't shoot arrows and throw spears at their own countrymen.

Siege Ramp

6. After several months of building the siege ramp, the Romans finally reached the top of Masada and severely damaged the exterior wall.
7. When the Jewish Zealots realized they were in grave danger of being conquered, they built another interior wall just inside the exterior wall using wood beams from many of their buildings.

They layered the beams with earth in between in order to fortify the new wall.

8. The Romans set this inner wall on fire and were now poised to enter. However, this all happened late at night, so the Romans decided to wait until the next morning to make their attack.
9. Eleazar Ben-Yair, the commander of the Zealots, gave an impassioned speech about how God had not created them to be slaves and about what would happen to them if they surrendered to the Romans. This is what he proposed:
   - The Romans are angry after the long battle and will kill most of us by torture. Those who are not killed will be mistreated and forced to be slaves. Our women will be raped before our eyes and violated, and our children will be tortured and forced to be slaves as well.
   - The only option we have as free people is to take our own lives.
   - So the men gathered in a special meeting and drew lots picking out 10 courageous men who knew about killing and understood how to die.
   - Then every father went home and killed their wives and children.
   - Then all the men gathered again together, and 10 of these men in the group killed the remaining men. Then one man killed the other 9, and then the last man killed himself.

Northern Palace

10. On May 3, 74 AD, after 7 months or so of long battled weariness, the Romans entered the top of Masada and stood in awe-stricken silence as they beheld the mass suicide of the Jews before them. The Zealots chose to die by suicide rather than be conquered by the Romans to be abused or killed.

Faith Lesson from Masada

1. While we don't endorse and believe the Jewish Zealots should have committed suicide as it's only God's place to take a person's life, we do understand these Zealots' decision.
2. While some of the Zealots may have believed in Christ and were devoted servants to God, the Jewish nation as a whole, and their leaders, had largely rejected Christ as their Messiah. As a result, Christ spoke judgment upon the nation in Luke 19:41–44.
3. Almost every instance in which a country falls, it's due mainly to the decisions of its leaders.
4. The sad reality is that the righteous always suffer at the hands of the wicked.
5. Today, it's the same; while there may be many righteous people in a country, God will still judge it because of the sinful and immoral decisions its leaders and the majority of the people make.

Cable cars headed up to Masada

6. Israel didn't return to be a nation again until 1948, and this was due to God's sovereign plan for them. God prophesied that He would bring them back again to be a nation, and it's a miracle that after almost 2,000 years, this has been fulfilled. This is unheard of in the history of any civilization.
7. However, the price Israel paid for their rejection of Christ cost them dearly and should be a sober warning to us today as well.

Journal/Notes:

Negev & Southern Israel Sites

Qumran and the Dead Sea Scrolls

Location

1. Qumran is located on the northwest side of the Dead Sea on Hwy. 90 about 13 miles (21 km.) east of Jerusalem.
2. It's in the Judean Wilderness, where it's barren and hot.
3. It's located 1200 ft. (366 m.) below sea level.
4. Its water source comes from the Judean Mountains to the west of the community via an aqueduct.
5. There are many caves in the area.
6. At Qumran, one of the most important discoveries in the history of biblical archaeology took place in around 1947.

Historical Background

1. It's believed the ancient settlement of Qumran was established by a Jewish group called the Essenes.
2. They lived here from about 200 BC to around 68 AD.
3. There were around 200 people who inhabited Qumran.
4. The ruins were excavated in the 1950s by a French archaeological team.
5. The Essenes were a spiritually devoted group of folks who left Jerusalem due to their belief that the priesthood had become corrupted beyond repair and separated themselves to study the Bible, copy it, and seek the Lord in the desert.
6. They were a strict Torah observant, Messianic, apocalyptic, new covenant Jewish sect. They were led by a priest they called the "Teacher of Righteousness." They were highly educated and very familiar with writing and study.
7. The future monastery lifestyle followed similar patterns of the

Essene community.

8. Josephus wrote that the men of Qumran rejected marriage, and instead, cared for the needy and neglected children of others. However, later discoveries have found skeletons of women, so it's believed some men possibly were married and that women were part of the community as well.
9. The Essenes most likely wrote the Dead Sea Scrolls from about 200 BC to 68 AD. Josephus and other secular sources mention the Essenes. However, they are not mentioned in the New Testament.
10. When the Essenes saw the nation of Israel falling to the Romans in around 68 AD, they hid their manuscripts in caves around Qumran. These manuscripts are what we refer to as the Dead Sea Scrolls.

Historical Background of the Dead Sea Scrolls

1. In around 1947, Bedouin shepherds were tending their goats and sheep near the ancient settlement of Qumran. One of the shepherds threw a rock into a cave and heard an echo sound. He and his friends later climbed into the cave and found a collection of large clay jars, seven of which contained leather and papyrus scrolls. An antiquities dealer from Bethlehem bought the scrolls, which later wound up in the possession of numerous scholars who estimated that the manuscripts were around 2,000 years old. After news of the discovery was made public, Bedouin treasure hunters and archaeologists discovered tens of thousands of additional scroll fragments from 10 nearby caves.

Qumran

2. The scrolls were discovered in eleven caves between the years of 1947 and 1956. The manuscripts are numbered according to the caves in which they were found.

3. There are around 972 manuscripts (15,000 fragments) that have been found to date. The longest is 26 ft. (8 m.) long.
4. They include fragments from every book of the Old Testament except for the Book of Esther (Esther might have been lost or decomposed due to time or may have been damaged by the Bedouin shepherds).
5. The writings consist of biblical manuscripts and other religious writings that circulated during the Second Temple era (516 BC to 70 AD). About 230 of the manuscripts are referred to as biblical scrolls. However, many of the manuscripts were fragmented and had to be assembled.

Qumran Caves

6. Cave 4, which is right beside ancient Qumran, had around 75% of all the material from the Qumran caves.
7. The Isaiah Scroll, found relatively intact, is 1,000 years older than any previously known copy of Isaiah, and the other scrolls are the oldest group of Old Testament manuscripts ever found.
8. The major intact manuscripts from Caves 1 and 11 were published by the late fifties and are now housed in the Shrine of the Book Museum in Jerusalem.
9. Recently, an additional cave (Cave 12) has been discovered, but no manuscripts have been found there yet.
10. Amazingly, the biblical manuscripts are virtually identical to the manuscripts we have today of the Old Testament part of the Bible. This proves God's ability to preserve His word through the ages.
11. Interestingly, the inhabitants of Qumran were either killed or fled, as no one ever came back to retrieve the scrolls.

Places of Interest

1. Aqueduct Entrance
2. Reservoirs
3. Cisterns
4. Tower
5. Kitchen
6. Scriptorium
7. Pottery Shop
8. Kiln
9. Mikvah (ritual bath)
10. Assembly Hall
11. Pantry
12. Animal Pen
13. Aqueduct

14. Cave viewing area (caves 4–10)
15. Caves 1, 2, 3, and 11 are located 1 mile (1.62 km.) north of Qumran.

16. Dead Sea

Qumran and the Bible

1. The Dead Sea Scrolls would have been the same Hebrew Bible that Christ and the apostles used.
2. The Hebrew Bible was divided into 3 sections: the Law (Torah), the Writings (Historical Books), and the Prophets (Major and Minor Prophets).
3. Christ gave full validity to the authority and accuracy of Scripture and used every section of it in His teachings. He repeatedly said, *"So that it might be fulfilled," "It is written," "Have you not read?"* and so forth.
4. Christ used the Old Testament to explain His purpose on earth.

    Luke 24:27: *And beginning with Moses and all the Prophets, he explained to them what was said in all the Scriptures concerning himself.*
5. In the New Testament, there are 850 quotes or references to the Old Testament.
6. The New Testament is built upon the Old Testament and cannot be fully understood without it.

The Uniqueness of the Bible

1. The Bible was written by 40 different authors on 3 different continents and written over a period of 1,600 years. Yet all the books of the Bible harmonize and keep the same themes like a puzzle pieced together in perfect harmony.
2. This harmony is a miracle in and of itself. For example, if an accident happened on a street corner and 10 witnesses were asked what they saw, there would be many different accounts or versions of the incident. However, this is not so with the Bible. It has one guiding theme despite having many authors writing over a long period of time on different continents.

The Bible Was Written and Preserved Supernaturally by God

1. 2 Timothy 3:16–17: *All Scripture is breathed out by God and profitable for teaching, for reproof, for correction, and for training in righteousness, 17 that the man of God may be competent, equipped for every good work.*
2. 2 Peter 1:19–21: *And we have something more sure, the prophetic word, to which you will do well to pay attention as to a lamp shining in a dark place, until the day dawns and the morning star rises in your hearts, 20 knowing this first of all, that no prophecy of Scripture comes from someone's own interpretation. 21 For no prophecy was ever produced by the will of man, but men spoke from God as they were carried along by the Holy Spirit.*

Qumran

3. Hebrews 4:12–13: *For the word of God is living and active, sharper than any two-edged sword, piercing to the division of soul and of spirit, of joints and of marrow, and discerning the thoughts and intentions of the heart. 13 And no creature is hidden from his sight, but all are naked and exposed to the eyes of him to whom we must*

give account.

4. Matthew 4:4: *But he answered, "It is written, 'Man shall not live by bread alone, but by every word that comes from the mouth of God.'"*
5. Matthew 5:18: *For truly, I say to you, until heaven and earth pass away,* **not an iota, not a dot***, will pass from the Law until all is accomplished.*
6. Luke 21:33: *Heaven and earth will pass away, but* **my words** *will not pass away.*

Faith Lesson from Qumran

1. The Dead Sea Scrolls were one of the most important discoveries in the history of mankind. God supernaturally allowed this in order to prove the reliability of His Word. Do we believe in the Bible and that it's God's divine revelation to us?
2. Christ referred to every section of the Hebrew Bible (Old Testament) and repeatedly said, *"So that it might be fulfilled," "It is written," "Have you not read?"* and so forth. If Christ claimed the Hebrew Bible of His day was accurate, do we trust in the accuracy of the Bible we have today as well?
3. The New Testament contains around 850 references from the Old Testament. This shows how the New Testament is built upon the Old Testament. Do we read the Old Testament in order to understand the New Testament better?
4. If Christ was so passionate about the truthfulness of Scripture and claimed it was the very Word of God, then we too, like Christ, can certainly trust God's ability to preserve Scripture. Like Christ, are we passionate about the Bible, and do we read it regularly?
5. If God supernaturally preserved the accuracy of the Old Testament, do we believe He could do the same for the New Testament?

Journal/Notes:

Sodom and Gomorrah

Location

1. Sodom and Gomorrah are located on the eastern side of the Dead Sea.
2. Gomorrah is situated at the base of Masada, and Sodom is about 13 miles (20 km.) south of Gomorrah.
3. Though the actual locations of the cities are somewhat disputed, growing evidence reveals that the locations are quite certain.

Historical Background

1. Josephus, a historian writer during the time of Christ, said the ruins could still be clearly seen in his day.
2. Archeologists have discovered around 1.5 million bodies in graves in these areas around Sodom and Gomorrah.
3. There are a lot of brimstone (old name for sulfur) balls in these cities.
4. This sulfur is unique and different from all other sulfur found in the world.
    - It's around 90-95% pure.
    - It's white, unlike any other place in the world.
    - It's so pure you can light it on fire, and it burns a hot blue flame.
    - These sulfur balls are not found between the cities.
5. There is a lot of ash in these areas that fits the biblical narrative.

    2 Peter 2:6: *And if He condemned the cities of **Sodom and Gomorrah** to destruction by **reducing them to ashes**, having made them an example to those who would live ungodly lives thereafter.*
6. The material of these city formations is calcium sulfate, which is what limestone and sulfur become when heated.

7. The preferred building material in Israel is limestone, so these cities fit the scientific evidence as well.
8. There is a lot of charcoal layers found in the strata of these cities.
9. The amount of ash, charcoal, and calcium sulfate reveal overwhelming evidence of extreme heat in these cities.
10. There is also no geothermal activity in these areas to explain the ash, charcoal, and calcium sulfate.
11. In addition, there are many unexplained shapes in these areas that look like buildings, Sphinxes, pyramids, and palaces.
12. These cities existed around 4,000 years ago, so their remains would be difficult to distinguish. Plus, God destroyed and reduced them to ashes as well.

Sphinx at Gomorrah

13. These cities fit the location as described in the Bible.

Genesis 13:10: *Lot lifted up his eyes and saw all the valley of the Jordan, that it was well watered everywhere—this was before the Lord destroyed Sodom and Gomorrah—like the garden of the Lord,* **like the land of Egypt as you go to Zoar** *[Zoar has been identified as being south of Sodom and Gomorrah].*

14. Because the Dead Sea basin used to be like the Garden of Eden, it was an extremely desirable climate that was great for agriculture and life in general. It was, therefore, a very populated area.
15. The thought of God raining down fire and brimstone upon the cities and people in this area is staggering and gives me chills up and down my spine. This fire and brimstone were so hot and intense they destroyed everything in its wake.
16. God also used Sodom and Gomorrah to refer to all of the cities of the Dead Sea basin.

Negev & Southern Israel Biblical Sites Guide

Places of Interest
1. Sodom
2. Gomorrah
3. Zoar
4. Admah
5. Zeboiim
6. Masada
7. Sphinx
8. Pyramid

Sodom and Gomorrah in the Bible

1. **God told Abraham through two angels about His plan to destroy Sodom and Gomorrah.**

   Genesis 18:20–21: *And the Lord said, "The outcry of **Sodom and Gomorrah** is indeed great, and their sin is exceedingly grave. 21 I will go down now and see if they have done entirely according to its outcry, which has come to Me; and if not, I will know."*

2. **During a dialogue between Abraham and God, Abraham pleaded with God to spare the cities on account of the righteous ones living in them (Gen. 18:22–31).**

3. **God told Abraham that He would spare the cities if only 10 righteous people could be found in them.**

   Genesis 18:32–33: *And He said, "I will not destroy it on account of the ten." 33 As soon as He had finished speaking to Abraham the Lord departed, and Abraham returned to his place.*

4. **In the cities of Sodom and Gomorrah lived hundreds of thousands of people. The fact that there were not even 10 righteous people speaks of the extreme wickedness of these cities.**

   Genesis 13:13: *Now the men of **Sodom were wicked exceedingly** and sinners against the Lord.*

5. **The wickedness of Sodom revealed.**

   Genesis 19:1–11: *Now the two angels came to **Sodom** in the evening as Lot was sitting in the gate of **Sodom**. When Lot saw them, he rose to meet them and bowed down with his face to the ground. 2 And he said, "Now behold, my lords, please turn aside into your servant's house, and spend the night, and wash your feet; then you may rise early and go on your way." They said however, "No, but we shall spend the night in the square." 3 Yet he urged them strongly, so they turned aside to him and entered his*

   Gomorrah

house; and he prepared a feast for them, and baked unleavened bread, and they ate. 4 Before they lay down, the men of the city, the men of **Sodom**, surrounded the house, both young and old, all the people from every quarter; 5 and they called to Lot and said to him, "Where are the men who came to you tonight? Bring them out to us that we **may have relations with them**." 6 But Lot went out to them at the doorway, and shut the door behind him, 7 and said, "Please, my brothers, do not act wickedly. 8 Now behold, I have two daughters who have not had relations with man; please let me bring them out to you, and do to them whatever you like; only do nothing to these men, inasmuch as they have come

under the shelter of my roof." 9 But they said, "Stand aside." Furthermore, they said, "This one came in as an alien, and already he is acting like a judge; now we will treat you worse than them." So they pressed hard against Lot and came near to break the door. 10 But the men [two angels] reached out their hands and brought Lot into the house with them, and shut the door. 11 They struck the men who were at the doorway of the house with blindness, both small and great, so that they wearied themselves trying to find the doorway.

6. **God warns Lot and his family to flee for their lives.**

Genesis 19:12–17: Then the two men said to Lot, "Whom else have you here? A son-in-law, and your sons, and your daughters, and whomever you have in the city, bring them out of the place; 13 for we are about to destroy this place, because their outcry has become so great before the Lord that the Lord has sent us to destroy it." 14 Lot went out and spoke to his sons-in-law, who were to marry his daughters, and said, "Up, get out of this place, for the Lord will destroy the city." But he appeared to his sons-in-law to be jesting. 15 When morning dawned, the angels urged Lot, saying, "Up, take your wife and your two daughters who are here, or you will be swept away in the punishment of the city." 16 But he hesitated. So the men

Negev & Southern Israel Sites

seized his hand and the hand of his wife and the hands of his two daughters, for the compassion of the Lord was upon him; and they brought him out, and put him outside the city. 17 When they had brought them outside, one [angel] said, "Escape for your life! Do not look behind you, and do not stay anywhere in the valley; escape to the mountains, or you will be swept away."

7. **God destroys Sodom and Gomorrah.**

   Genesis 19:23–29: *The sun had risen over the earth when Lot came to Zoar [located south of Sodom and Gomorrah]. 24 Then the Lord rained on **Sodom and Gomorrah** brimstone and fire from the Lord out of heaven, 25 and He overthrew those cities, and all the valley, and **all the inhabitants of the cities**, and what grew on the ground. 26 But his wife, from behind him, looked back, and she became a pillar of salt. 27 Now Abraham arose early in the morning and went to the place where he had stood before the Lord; 28 and he looked down toward **Sodom and Gomorrah**, and toward all the land of the valley, and he saw, and*

   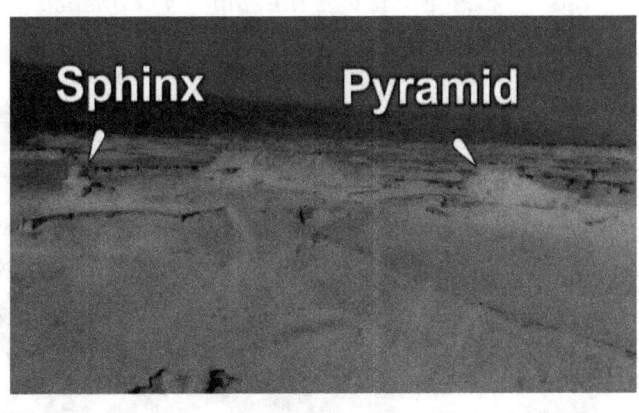

   *behold, the smoke of the land ascended like the smoke of a furnace. 29 Thus, it came about, when God destroyed the **cities of the valley**, that God remembered Abraham, and sent Lot out of the midst of the overthrow, when He overthrew the cities in which Lot lived.*

God uses Sodom and Gomorrah as examples of judgment upon the ungodly throughout the Bible.

1. **Moses used Sodom and Gomorrah as warnings for the future generations of the Israelites.**

   Deuteronomy 29:23: *All its land is brimstone and salt, a burning waste, unsown and unproductive, and no grass grows in it, like the overthrow of **Sodom** and **Gomorrah**, **Admah** and **Zeboiim**, which the Lord overthrew in His anger and in His wrath.*

   God specifically states that He destroyed two other cities besides

Sodom and Gomorrah (Admah and Zeboiim). However, it appears He also destroyed Zoar because after Lot left Zoar, his two daughters said there was no one in the land for them to marry.

2. **The prophets continually used Sodom and Gomorrah as examples of God's wrath on the ungodly.**

   Jeremiah 49:18: *"Like the overthrow of **Sodom and Gomorrah with its neighbors**,"* says the Lord, *"no one will live there, nor will a son of man reside in it."*

   Lamentations 4:6: *For the iniquity of the daughter of my people Is greater than the sin of **Sodom**, which was overthrown as in a moment, and no hands were turned toward her.*

3. **Jesus used Sodom and Gomorrah as examples of God's judgment on the ungodly.**

   Luke 17:28–30: *It was the same as happened in the days of Lot: they were eating, they were drinking, they were buying, they were selling, they were planting, 29 they were building; but on the day that Lot went out from **Sodom** it rained fire and brimstone from heaven and destroyed them all. 30 It will be just the same on the day that the Son of Man is revealed.*

   Gomorrah

4. **The Apostles used Sodom and Gomorrah as examples of God's coming judgment on the ungodly.**

   2 Peter 2:4–10: *For if God did not spare angels when they sinned, but cast them into hell and committed them to pits of darkness, reserved for judgment; 5 and did not spare the ancient world, but preserved Noah, a preacher of righteousness, with seven others, when He brought a flood upon the world of the ungodly; 6 and if He condemned the cities of **Sodom and Gomorrah** to destruction by reducing them to ashes, having made them **an example** to those who would live ungodly lives thereafter; 7 and if He rescued*

righteous Lot, oppressed by the sensual conduct of unprincipled men 8 (for by what he saw and heard that righteous man, while living among them, felt his righteous soul tormented day after day by their lawless deeds), 9 then the Lord knows how to rescue the godly from temptation, and to keep the unrighteous under punishment for the day of judgment, 10 and especially those who indulge the flesh in its corrupt desires and despise authority.

Jude 1:5–7: *Now I want to remind you, although you once fully knew it, that Jesus, who saved a people out of the land of Egypt, afterward destroyed those who did not believe. 6 And the angels who did not stay within their own position of authority, but left their proper dwelling, he has kept in eternal chains under gloomy darkness until the judgment of the great day— 7 just as* **Sodom and Gomorrah and the surrounding cities**, *which likewise indulged in* **sexual immorality and pursued unnatural desire**, *serve as an example by undergoing a punishment of eternal fire.*

Sulfur balls at Sodom and Gomorrah

Repeatedly, throughout the accounts of the destruction of Sodom and Gomorrah, the sin of homosexuality is highlighted as the main wickedness for which God destroyed them.

Some, who defend homosexuality, claim that God destroyed them because of their lack of hospitality.

5. **God uses the same imagery of fire and brimstone in the destruction of Sodom and Gomorrah as for what hell will be like.**

Revelation 20:10: *And the devil who deceived them was thrown into the lake of* **fire and brimstone**, *where the beast and the false prophet are also; and they will be tormented day and night forever and ever.*

Faith Lesson from Sodom and Gomorrah

1. The lesson from Sodom and Gomorrah is a serious, sobering message we should allow to sink in deeply.
2. The primary sin for which God destroyed Sodom and Gomorrah was homosexuality. However, they sinned in many other ways as well.
3. Sodom and Gomorrah are a foreshadow of what hell will be like.
4. Jesus talked about how His second coming would be like that of Sodom and Gomorrah. Jesus also spoke more about hell than heaven.
5. If God, the prophets, Christ, and the apostles used Sodom and Gomorrah as an example of the eternal judgment in hell that awaits the ungodly, then we should do the same today as well.

Burning sulfur ball – Copyright Discovered Media

6. God is a God of love and has done everything He can to save us, but for those who reject His offer of salvation, eternal suffering in the Lake of Fire awaits them (Rev. 20:10).

Journal/Notes:

St. George's Monastery

Location

1. St. George's Monastery is located about 2.5 miles (4 km.) west of Jericho in a deep and breathtaking gorge called "Wadi Qelt."
2. It's located on the ancient road connecting the Jordan Valley to Jerusalem and beyond. Jesus would have used this well-traveled road regularly.
3. The story of the Good Samaritan took place on this road. (For more on this story and event, please see the Inn of the Good Samaritan.)

Historical Background

1. St. George's Monastery is a Greek Orthodox cliff-hanging complex carved into a sheer rock wall in the Judaean Desert and is one of the most breathtaking sights in the Holy Land.
2. Starting in the 4th century, monks began to live in the many caves of Wadi Qelt.
3. The monastery of St. George was founded in the 5th century by John of Thebes, an Egyptian. He gathered a small band of five Syrian hermits who had settled around the cave where they believed the prophet Elijah was fed by ravens (1 Kings 17:1–7).
4. Tradition also holds that Elijah visited the cave by the monastery while traveling to the Sinai Peninsula as he fled the threats of Jezebel after he had killed the false prophets of Baal and Asherah (1 Kings 19:1–3).
5. However, it was named after its most famous monk, St George of Koziba, who came as a teenager from Cyprus in the 6th century to follow the ascetic life in the Holy Land after his parents died.
6. The monastery was destroyed in 614 AD by the Persians and was more or less abandoned after the Persians swept through the

valley and massacred the fourteen monks who dwelt there. The bones and skulls of the martyred monks can still be seen today in the monastery chapel.

7. The Crusaders made some attempts at restoration of the monastery in 1179 AD. However, it was abandoned after Muslims regained control of the Holy Land and drove out the Crusaders.

St. George's Monastery from lookout point

8. In 1878, a Greek monk, Kalinikos, settled here and restored the monastery, finishing it in 1901.

History of Christian Monasticism

1. Today, in Israel, there are 33 functioning monasteries. During the 4th century, there were hundreds of monasteries built as almost every holy site had a monastery on it.
2. Because Christianity was prohibited in the Roman Empire before Constantine embraced Christianity, no monasteries or churches were permitted until 313 AD. After this point, monasteries sprung up everywhere throughout the empire.
3. The idea of a monastic lifestyle was taken from both the Old and New Testaments.
    - The Nazarite Vow
    - The prophets (Elijah being fed by ravens in the desert).
    - John the Baptist living in the desert.
    - Christ fasting for 40 days in the desert.
4. There were also the Essenes who lived in the desert by the Dead Sea at Qumran during the time of John the Baptist and Jesus.
5. Monasticism took on different forms and meanings throughout its history.

- Some lived like hermits all alone.
- Later, many lived in monasteries in communal groups.
- They withdrew from society to live a separated life fully devoted to seeking the Lord and becoming godly.
- Over the years, monasticism changed so that many monasteries prepared men and women for a life of service to God. They would live in the monastery for a few years then go out to serve the Lord.
- Monasteries were not always Catholic. There were many monasteries before Catholicism became what it is today, and there were different kinds of monasteries from different religious orientations, i.e., Greek Orthodox, Russian Orthodox, Armenian, etc.

6. In general, monasticism is a religious way of life wherein a person denounces worldly pursuits and fully devotes themselves to seeking the Lord through religious vows and disciplines.
7. The word monk, or monastery, originates from Greek (monos) and means to "dwell alone."
8. In different periods of monasticism, some chose lives of celibacy as well.

Places of Interest

1. St. George's Monastery – It is quite a hike down into the gorge to see the monastery, so only those in good physical shape should attempt it. It can also be extremely hot during the summer.
2. Lookout – Just to the west of the parking area is a trail that leads to a beautiful lookout area over the monastery for those just wanting to see the site without hiking down to it.
3. Monastery Upper Level – Elijah's Cave

4. Monastery Middle Level – Main Church
5. Monastery Lower Level – Storehouses and vault where the remains of the early monks are kept.
6. Stairs from the inner court of the monastery lead to the cave-church of St. Elijah. From this cave, a narrow tunnel provides an escape route to the top of the mountain.
7. Wadi Qelt – Fertile ravine where small-scale farming and irrigation takes place.
8. Caves where monks lived.
9. Small Chapel

St. George's Monastery in the Bible

1. **It seems very unlikely that St. George's Monastery is the location where God supernaturally fed Elijah by ravens. The Bible says the place was east of the Jordan River, and St. George's Monastery is west of the Jordan River.**

    1 Kings 17:1–7: Now Elijah the Tishbite, of Tishbe in Gilead, said to Ahab, "As the Lord, the God of Israel, lives, before whom I stand, there shall be neither dew nor rain these years, except by my word." 2 And the word of the Lord came to him: 3 "Depart from here and turn eastward and hide yourself by the brook Cherith, **which is east of the Jordan***. 4 You shall drink from the brook, and I have commanded the ravens to feed you there." 5 So he went and did according to the word of the Lord. He*

Walkway down to St. George's Monastery

went and lived by the brook Cherith that is **east of the Jordan***. 6 And the ravens brought him bread and meat in the morning, and bread and meat in the evening, and he drank from the brook. 7 And after a while the brook dried up, because there was no rain in the land.*

2. **It is possible Elijah stayed in the cave at St. George's Monastery when he fled after being threatened by Jezebel, but it's not certain.**

   1 Kings 19:3: *Then he was afraid, and he arose and ran for his life and came to Beersheba, which belongs to Judah, and left his servant there.*

Faith Lesson from St. George's Monastery

1. We can certainly admire those who took God so seriously that they often sold their possessions and chose a life of solitude and strict discipline to seek the Lord. Do we love the Lord to such a degree we are willing to give up whatever God might ask us so we can be more devoted followers of Him?
2. Do we set time aside to remove the distractions of life and just seek God?
3. While it's good to set time apart for solitude and seeking the Lord, we are also called to be in the world but not of it. Are we doing a good job of being in the world but not a part of its values and

philosophies?
4. Are we disciplined in our Christian lives?
5. While monasticism has many admirable qualities, it does have some unbiblical concepts. For some, it was a withdrawal and escape from society. Like Christ, we are called to influence society and be lights to the world. Are we influencing those around us with the light of God's Word and His love? And are we fulfilling the Great Commission in one way or another?

Wadi Qelt and St. George's Monastery

6. Are we part of a Bible-believing church community where we can grow and serve others?

Journal/Notes:

Negev & Southern Israel Sites

Timna Park: Tabernacle Replica

Location

1. Timna Park is 17 miles (27 km.) north of Eilat and the Red Sea, on Hwy. 90.
2. Located within Timna Park is another park that has an exact replica of the tabernacle God ordered Moses to build while he was on Mount Sinai.
3. This tabernacle contains every piece of furniture, Brazen Altar, Table of Shewbread, Ark of the Covenant, and everything the original tabernacle had. It's the only life-size model of its kind in Israel that is exactly like the original one. It has been researched extensively and built according to the specifications given to Moses.
4. Timna Park is in the arid desert of Arava and is on the route the Israelites would have taken in their travels. It's not for certain, but it's possible the Israelites could have camped in the same area.
5. The landscape around Timna Park is very similar to that of biblical times when the children of Israel wandered in the desert for 40 years. The arid country, lack of water, and heat all paint a picture of what it would have been like to live in the desert at that time.

Historical Background

1. The tabernacle was portable, and its specifications are found in Exodus chapters 25–40.
2. Most Christians skim over or don't read the sections and books of the Bible that deal with the details of the Law and the tabernacle.
3. Some might wonder why God spent 40 days instructing Moses about the tabernacle but only spent 6 days creating the entire universe?
4. And if God only needed a little over one chapter to describe the

structure of the world, why did He need 15 chapters to describe the design and details of the tabernacle?

5. For most Christians, reading from Genesis to Exodus chapter 20 is great. Then, they get bogged down in the rest of Exodus, Leviticus, and part of Numbers.
6. The fact that God spends so much time on the details of how mankind can be right with Him reveals that He is more concerned about having a relationship with us than the importance of His creation.

Places of Interest

1. Tabernacle Courtyard Fence
   - It measures 75 ft. wide (23 m.) by 150 ft. long (46 m.).
   - The Courtyard has 60 posts with linen curtains all around it.
   - The Courtyard posts were 7.5 ft. high (2.29 m.).
   - Each post had a bronze base with silver hooks and rings on top.
   - Acacia wood was used for the tabernacle. These trees can be seen close to the tabernacle in Timna Park today.
   - The Eastern Gate, which was the entrance, had 4 posts and a colored curtain.

Negev & Southern Israel Sites

2. Courtyard
   - The Bronze (copper) Altar measured 7.5 ft. wide square (2.29 m.) by 4.5 ft. high (1.37 m.) and had 4 horns on each corner (also called the horns of the altar).
   - The Bronze Laver or washbasin made from brass.
   - Sacrifices and cleansing took place in the courtyard outside the Holy Place. Judgment and cleansing had to take place first before the priests could enter the tabernacle or temple.
3. The Tabernacle (also known as the tent of meeting)
   - It measured 45 ft. long (13.72 m.) by 15 ft. wide by 15 ft. high (4.57 m.).
   - It was made with 10 curtains of fine linen of blue, purple, and scarlet yarn.
   - Each curtain was made with an embroidered cherub.
4. The Holy Place
   - Only the priests and High Priest could enter the Holy Place.
   - It measured 15 ft. wide (4.57 m.) by 30 ft. long (9.14 m.).
   - It contained the Menorah made from a single piece of gold.
   - The Table of Showbread (representing the unleavened bread of the first Passover) measured 36 inches wide (91.44 cm.) by 18 inches deep (45.72 cm.) by 27 inches tall (68.58 cm.). On it

were 12 loaves of bread which represented the 12 tribes of Israel.
- The Altar of Incense measured 18 inches square (45.72 cm.) by 36 inches tall (91.44 cm.). Only a special kind of incense was to be burned upon it.
- The priests wore white linen robes with a colorful sash.
- The High Priest wore special garments (a turban, ephod, breastplate, and robe). The breastplate contained 12 stones, each representing the 12 tribes of Israel. There were bells and pomegranates at the bottom of the robe.

5. The Veil Curtain separated the Holy Place from the Holy of Holies. It was made of blue, purple, and scarlet thread.
6. The Holy of Holies.
   - It measured 15 ft. by 15 ft. (4.6 m. by 4.6 m.).
   - Only the High Priest could enter the Holy of Holies once a year on the day of Yom Kippur, and he wore a holy linen coat (Lev. 16:4).
   - He had to be purified from all sin before entering.
   - Tradition holds that a rope was tied to the waist of the High Priest in case God smote him for being impure in His sight. By doing so, he could be drug out with the rope because they were forbidden to enter the Holy of Holies. This tradition might very well be true, but it's not mentioned in the Bible.

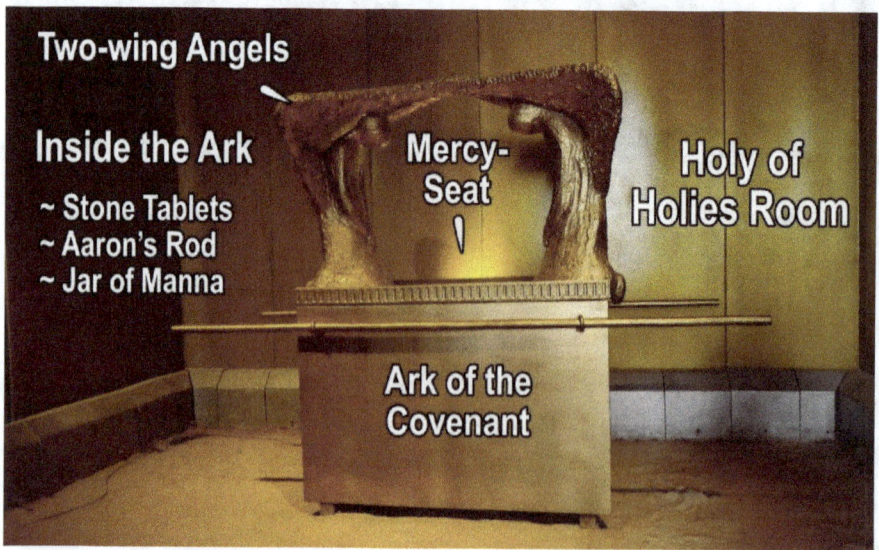

- Inside the Holy of Holies was the Ark of the Covenant, which measured 45 inches wide (114 cm.) by 27 inches deep by 27 inches tall (68.58 cm.).
- On top of the Ark of the Covenant was the Mercy Seat, which measured 27 inches high (68.58 cm.). Molded to it were 2-winged cherubim angel figures made from one piece of gold.
- Inside the Ark of the Covenant were the Ten Commandments written on Stone Tablets by the finger of God, Aaron's Rod that budded, and a Jar of Manna.

Tabernacle in the Bible

1. **God gave the instructions of how to build the tabernacle to Moses while he was on Mount Sinai.**

   Exodus 24:15–18: *Then Moses went up on the mountain, and the cloud covered the mountain. 16 The glory of the Lord dwelt on Mount Sinai, and the cloud covered it six days. And on the seventh day he called to Moses out of the midst of the cloud. 17 Now the appearance of the glory of the Lord was like a devouring fire on the top of the mountain in the sight of the people of Israel. 18 Moses entered the cloud and went up on the mountain. And Moses was on the mountain forty days and forty nights.*

   Mount Sinai with blackened top

   Hebrews 8:5: *They serve a copy and shadow of the heavenly things. For when Moses was about to erect the tent, he was instructed by God, saying, "See that you make everything according to the pattern that was shown you on the mountain."*

2. **The tabernacle was to be God's special dwelling place among His people.**

Exodus 25:1–9: *The Lord said to Moses, 2 "Speak to the people of Israel, that they take for me a contribution. From every man whose heart moves him you shall receive the contribution for me. 3 And this is the contribution that you shall receive from them: gold, silver, and bronze, 4 blue and purple and scarlet yarns and fine twined linen, goats' hair, 5 tanned rams' skins, goatskins, acacia wood, 6 oil for the lamps, spices for the anointing oil and for the fragrant incense, 7 onyx stones, and stones for setting, for the ephod and for the breastpiece. 8 And let them* **make me a sanctuary, that I may dwell in their midst**. *9 Exactly as I show you concerning the pattern of the tabernacle, and of all its furniture, so you shall make it."*

3. **The presence of God was over the tabernacle in the form of a cloud by day and fire by night.**

   Numbers 9:15–17: *On the day that the tabernacle was set up, the* **cloud covered the tabernacle**, *the tent of the testimony. And at evening it was over the tabernacle like the appearance of fire until morning. 16 So it was always: the* **cloud covered it by day and the appearance of fire by night**. *17 And whenever the cloud lifted from over the tent, after that the people of Israel set out, and in the place where the cloud settled down, there the people of Israel camped.*

   Tabernacle replica at Timna Park

4. **Part of the reason the Levites were chosen to be the priests and servants of the temple was because of the zeal for the Lord they displayed regarding the Golden Calf at Mount Sinai.**

   Exodus 32:25–29: *And when Moses saw that the people had broken loose (for Aaron had let them break loose, to the derision of their enemies), 26 then Moses stood in the gate of the camp and said, "Who is on the Lord's side? Come to me." And all the* **sons of Levi gathered around him**. *27 And he said to them, "Thus says the Lord*

*God of Israel, 'Put your sword on your side each of you, and go to and fro from gate to gate throughout the camp, and each of you kill his brother and his companion and his neighbor.'" 28 And the sons of Levi did according to the word of Moses. And that day about three thousand men of the people fell. 29 And Moses said, "**Today you have been ordained for the service of the Lord**, each one at the cost of his son and of his brother, so that he might bestow a blessing upon you this day."*

Faith Lesson from the Tabernacle

1. God focused on the details of the tabernacle because He wanted to embed some essential concepts in our minds.
2. The details of the tabernacle reveal how sinful people must approach a holy God.
3. The tabernacle was God's special dwelling place among mankind.
4. The tabernacle and sacrificial system details reveal that God is more concerned about having a relationship with us than His creation.
5. It reveals the honor and respect we should have toward God.
6. The tabernacle and sacrificial system show the consequences of sin and the value of Christ's sacrifice on the Cross. When a person sinned in the Old Testament, it cost them financially as they had to offer a sacrifice from their flocks or purchase one.

Tabernacle courtyard with altar and laver basin

7. The tabernacle was a pattern of heavenly things.

   Hebrews 8:5–6: *They serve a copy and shadow of the heavenly things. For when Moses was about to erect the tent, he was instructed by God, saying, "See that you make everything according to the pattern that was shown you on the mountain." 6 But as it is, Christ has obtained a ministry that is as much more excellent than* the old as the covenant he mediates is better, since it is enacted on better promises.

8. The tabernacle gives insight and understanding regarding the privilege believers have today of being the temple of the living God.

   1 Corinthians 3:16–17: *Do you not know that you are a **temple of God** and that the Spirit of God dwells in you? 17 If any man destroys the temple of God, God will destroy him, for the **temple of God is holy, and that is what you are**.*

9. The concepts of the tabernacle provide understanding for believers today about how we are a living temple made with living stones.

   Inside the Ark of the Covenant

   1 Peter 2:4–5: *And coming to Him as to a living stone which has been rejected by men, but is choice and precious in the sight of God, 5 you also, as living stones, are being built up as a **spiritual house** for a **holy priesthood**, to offer up **spiritual sacrifices** acceptable to God through **Jesus Christ**.*

10. Those who skim over or neglect to read the details in Exodus, Leviticus, and Numbers will miss the foundational truths of who Christ is and what He did in redeeming us through His work on the Cross.

11. The New Testament is built upon the foundation of the Old Testament. Therefore, if our understanding of the Old Testament is weak, so will be our understanding of the New Testament.

Journal/Notes:

Valley of Elah

Location

1. The Valley of Elah is about 15 miles (23 km.) west of Bethlehem and about 20 miles (32 km.) east of the Mediterranean Sea.
2. It's located on the western edge of the Judean lower hills and was an important travel route from the coastal cities up to the center of the land of Judah and its main cities of Bethlehem, Jerusalem, and Hebron.

3. It's an undeveloped site that can be seen in its natural state. It has parking alongside Hwy. 38.
4. The Valley of Elah is best known for the epic battle between young David and the giant, Goliath, a skilled veteran warrior.

Historical Background

1. The Philistines were a Canaanite people who inhabited Israel before the Israelites arrived.
2. The Israelites were unable to conquer them, and there were battles between the two nations for much of Israel's history.
3. The Philistine's stronghold was on the coastal plain in the Gaza area.
4. They were powerful, cultured, and possessed iron. They were the high-tech people of the day and did all they could to prohibit Israel from gaining iron and access to their technology (1 Sam. 13:19).
5. They worshiped many false gods.
6. At this time in Israel's history, the Philistines were attempting to push up through the Valley of Elah towards the heart of Judah. King Saul and his army engaged with the Philistines to stop them.
7. The battle was one of the most pivotal between the two nations,

with the loser agreeing to serve the winner. It was a "winner takes all" kind of battle.

8. Later, King Saul would be killed by the Philistines in the Gilboa area.
9. David would eventually subdue the Philistines, and during the time of Solomon, there was peace between the two nations.
10. David was probably around 16–18 years old when he fought Goliath. We'll see why this is so as the story unfolds.

Places of Interest

1. Israelite Camp
2. Philistine Camp at Ephes-dammin
3. Valley of Elah
4. Azekah
5. Socoh
6. HaEla Stream – Place where David selected 5 smooth stones.
7. Battle Location
8. King David's Palace – Built by David when he became King as a memorial to his victory.

Valley of Elah in the Bible

1. **The battlefield setting.**

   1 Samuel 17:1–3: *Now the Philistines gathered their armies for battle. And they were gathered at **Socoh**, which belongs to Judah, and encamped between **Socoh** and **Azekah**, in **Ephes-dammim**. 2 And Saul and the men of Israel were gathered, and encamped in the **Valley of Elah**, and drew up in line of battle against the Philistines. 3 And the Philistines stood on the mountain on the one side, and Israel stood on the mountain on the other side, **with a valley between them**.*

2. **The battle terms defined.**

   1 Samuel 17:4–10: *And there came out from the camp of the Philistines a champion named Goliath of Gath, whose height was six cubits and a span [more than 9 ft., 2.74 m. tall]. 5 He had a helmet of bronze on his head, and he was armed with a coat of mail [bronze scale armor], and the weight of the coat was five thousand*

   *shekels of bronze [about 125 lbs., 57 kg.]. 6 And he had bronze armor on his legs, and a javelin of bronze slung between his shoulders. 7 The shaft of his spear was like a weaver's beam, and his spear's head weighed six hundred shekels of iron [15 lbs., 7 kg.]. And his shield-bearer went before him. 8 He stood and shouted to the ranks of Israel, "Why have you come out to draw up for battle? Am I not a Philistine, and are you not servants of Saul? Choose a man for yourselves and let him come down to me. 9 **If he is able to fight with me and kill me, then we will be your servants. But if I prevail against him and kill him, then you shall be our servants and serve us**." 10 And the Philistine said, "I defy the ranks of Israel this day. Give me a man, that we may fight together."*

3. **The hearts of the Israelites were jolted to their core, and they**

became terrified.

1 Samuel 17:11: *When Saul and all Israel heard these words of the Philistine, they were **dismayed and greatly afraid**.*

4. **David arrived at the Valley of Elah and accepted the challenge to fight Goliath.**

   1 Samuel 17:20–27: *And David rose early in the morning and left the sheep with a keeper and took the provisions and went, as Jesse had commanded him. And he came to the encampment as the host was going out to the battle line, shouting the war cry. 21 And Israel and the Philistines drew up for battle, army against army. 22 And David left the things in charge of the keeper of the baggage and ran to the ranks and went and greeted his brothers. 23 As he talked with them, behold, the champion, the Philistine of Gath, Goliath by name, came up out of the ranks of the Philistines and spoke the same words as before. And David heard*

   Stream where David picked up 5 smooth stones

   *him. 24 All the men of Israel, when they saw the man, **fled from him and were much afraid**. 25 And the men of Israel said, "Have you seen this man who has come up? Surely he has come up to defy Israel. And the king will enrich the man who kills him with great riches and will give him his daughter and make his father's house free in Israel." 26 And David said to the men who stood by him, "What shall be done for the man who kills this Philistine and takes away the reproach from Israel? For who is this uncircumcised Philistine, that he should defy the armies of the living God?" 27 And the people answered him in the same way, "So shall it be done to the man who kills him."*

5. **King Saul reluctantly agreed to allow David to fight Goliath.**

   1 Samuel 17:31–37: *When the words that David spoke were heard, they repeated them before Saul, and he sent for him. 32 And David said to Saul, "Let no man's heart fail because of him. Your servant*

*will go and fight with this Philistine." 33 And Saul said to David, "You are not able to go against this Philistine to fight with him, for **you are but a youth**, and he has been a **man of war from his youth**." 34 But David said to Saul, "Your servant used to keep sheep for his father. And when there came a lion, or a bear, and took a lamb from the flock, 35 I went after him and struck him and delivered it out of his mouth. And if he arose against me, I caught him by his beard and struck him and killed him. 36 Your servant has struck down both lions and bears, and this uncircumcised Philistine shall be like one of them, for he has defied the armies of the living God." 37 And David said, "The LORD who delivered me from the paw of the lion and from the paw of the bear will deliver me from the hand of this Philistine." And Saul said to David, "Go, and the LORD be with you!"*

View of Elah Valley from the Israelite camp

6. **David chose not to use King Saul's armor in the battle with Goliath.**

    1 Samuel 17:38–39: *Then Saul clothed David with his armor. He put a helmet of bronze on his head and clothed him with a coat of mail, 39 and David strapped his sword over his armor. And he tried in vain to go, for he had not tested them. Then David said to Saul, "**I cannot go with these, for I have not tested them**." So David put them off.*

7. **David, with just 5 smooth stones and a sling, went into battle against a heavily armed, experienced fighting machine, who was a giant of a man and had his armor-bearer with him.**

    1 Samuel 17:40–47: *Then he took his staff in his hand and **chose five smooth stones from the brook** and put them in his shepherd's pouch. His **sling was in his hand**, and he approached the Philistine. 41 And the Philistine moved forward and came near to David, **with his shield-bearer in front of him**. 42 And when the Philistine looked and saw David, he disdained him, for he was but a youth, ruddy and handsome in appearance. 43 And the Philistine said to*

David, "Am I a dog, that you come to me with sticks?" And the Philistine cursed David by his gods. 44 The Philistine said to David, "Come to me, and I will give your flesh to the birds of the air and to the beasts of the field." 45 Then David said to the Philistine, "You come to me with a sword and with a spear and with a javelin, but I come to you in the name of the LORD of hosts, the God of the armies of Israel, whom you have defied. 46 This day the LORD will deliver you into my hand, and I will strike you down and cut off your head. And I will give the dead bodies of the host of the Philistines this day to the birds of the air and to the wild beasts of the earth, **that all the earth may know that there is a God in Israel**, 47 and that all this assembly may

View of Elah Valley from the Philistine camp

know that the LORD saves not with sword and spear. For the **battle is the LORD's**, and he will give you into our hand."

8. **The outcome of the epic battle showdown.**

   1 Samuel 17:48–51: *When the Philistine arose and came and drew near to meet David, David ran quickly toward the battle line to meet the Philistine. 49 And David put his hand in his bag and took out a stone and slung it and struck the Philistine on his forehead. The stone sank into his forehead, and he fell on his face to the ground. 50 So David prevailed over the Philistine* **with a sling and with a stone**, *and struck the Philistine and killed him. There was no sword in the hand of David. 51 Then David ran and stood over the Philistine and took his sword and drew it out of its sheath and killed him and cut off his head with it.*

9. **David's defeat of Goliath led to a great victory over the Philistines.**

   1 Samuel 17:51–52: *When the Philistines saw that their champion was dead, they fled. 52 And the men of Israel and Judah rose with a shout and pursued the Philistines as far as Gath and the gates of Ekron, so that the wounded Philistines fell on the way from Shaaraim as far as Gath and Ekron.*

Faith Lesson from the Valley of Elah

1. The outcome of the battle was far more significant than we might realize. If the Israelites lost, they would become the servants of the Philistines. It was a "winner takes all" battle.

2. David's motivation in the battle was the glory of God and the protection of His name: *"So that all the earth may know that there is a God in Israel"* (1 Sam. 17:46).

3. During David's youth as a shepherd, he developed many skills. He learned music, how to write, use a sling, how to fight to protect his sheep, and how to love the Lord and obey Him.

4. God used David's skill of using a sling, along with his love for the Lord, to defeat Goliath.

5. The skills David developed as a youth he used throughout his life. He faithfully led the nation Israel, instilled a love for the Lord in his kingdom, and wrote many psalms that were used in his time and throughout history to this day.

6. David knew that it's not the size of our weapons but the size of our faith in God that matters. So he went into the battle full of faith, and confident God would give him the victory.

7. Do I understand that it's my responsibility to develop my abilities and God's responsibility to direct me in how I use them?

8. Do I realize that the most important skill I possess is my love for the Lord and my heart to obey Him?

9. What miracles might God want to do in my life that would show the whole earth that there is a God in the land?

Journal/Notes:

Other Sites in Southern Israel

Ashdod (Azotos)

Ashdod is a coastal city on the Mediterranean Sea about 18 miles (29 km.) south of Jaffa and Tel Aviv.

It was one of the 5 main stronghold cities of the Philistines and was well-fortified.

Ancient Ashdod

During the conquest of the Promised Land under Joshua and the Israelites, giants known as Anakim were found here (Josh. 11:22). Ashdod was allotted to Judah, but they failed to conquer it (Josh. 13:3, 15:46–47).

During the time of Samuel, Ashdod, and the other main cities of the Philistines were still independent

When the Israelites were defeated in battle under the priesthood of Eli and his wicked sons (Hophni and Phinehas), the ark was taken to the house of Dagon in Ashdod (1 Sam. 5:1–2). Later, it would be returned to the Israelites at Beth-Shemesh.

Ashdod was conquered and came under the authority of Assyria in around 711 BC. Later, Babylon conquered it as well in around 605 BC.

Ashdod was the recipient of many prophecies proclaiming its doom and destruction, i.e., Isaiah 20:11, Amos 1:8, Jeremiah 25:20, and Zechariah 2:4, 9:6. However, Ashdod continued to be inhabited as the Jews intermarried with its inhabitants after returning from Babylon (Neh. 13:23–24).

In the New Testament, Ashdod is called Azotus.

Acts 8:40: *But Philip found himself at **Azotus**, and as he passed through, he preached the gospel to all the towns until he came to Caesarea.*

Ashkelon

Ashkelon is a coastal city on the Mediterranean Sea about 27 miles (43 km.) south of Jaffa and Tel Aviv. It's also just a bit north of modern-day Gaza.

Ashkelon was one of the 5 main coastal cities of the Philistines.

Joshua and the Israelites conquered Ashkelon in the conquest of the Promised Land (Josh. 13:3), and it was allotted to Judah, who then occupied it (Judg. 1:18).

One of the golden tumors (emerods) that was returned with the Ark of the Covenant by the Philistines was from Ashkelon (1 Sam. 6:17).

Ruins at Ashkelon

Both Ashkelon and Gath are mentioned in David's lament over Saul and Jonathan, revealing their importance (2 Sam. 1:20).

Ashkelon is also mentioned with Gaza, Ashdod, and Ekron, in the prophet Amos' denunciations of their sin and coming judgment (Amos 1:7–8).

Ashkelon was also denounced by Jeremiah (Jer. 25:20, 47:5–7), Zephaniah (2:4–7), and Zechariah (9:5).

Bethany Beyond the Jordan

Tradition and archaeology hold that this site is the believed location of Bethany Beyond the Jordan. It's located on a tributary that connects to the Jordan River known as Wadi Kharrar. Just before the place this wadi joins the Jordan River is called Bethany Beyond the Jordan.

It's also just across from Qasr al-Yahud Baptismal Site on Israel's side of the river. (For more on Qasr al-Yahud Baptismal Site, please see Jordan River Baptismal Site of Jesus.)

Ancient baptismal site at Bethany Beyond the Jordan

This area is where Jesus is believed to have been baptized by John the Baptist (John 1:28), where John baptized many people, and where John lived for periods of time. It's on the Jordanian side of the Jordan River and consists of two distinct areas: Tell Al-Kharrar, also known as Jabal Mar-Elias (Elijah's Hill), and the area of the churches of John the Baptist. There are Roman and Byzantine ruins of churches, chapels, a monastery, caves that hermits have used, and pools in which baptisms were held.

Excavations at this site began in 1996, following Jordan's peace treaty with Israel in 1994, and have uncovered more than 20 churches, caves, and baptismal pools, all dating from the Roman and Byzantine periods.

This area is also associated with the ascension of the Prophet Elijah into heaven, which is commemorated at a hill called Tell Mar Elias or Jabal Mar-Elias (Elijah's Hill).

Dead Sea

What would a trip to Israel be without taking a dip in the famous Dead Sea? Following is some helpful info for helping you decide which beach is best for you.

Northern Beaches

The northern beaches are privately owned and charge a fee to enter, even if your stay is for a quick dip in the sea. They have more of the mud for skincare, the water is a little cooler, they have higher waves and a little less salt content. However, there is still plenty of salt, so you can float quite easily.

For health reasons, a strong warning is given regarding swallowing the saltwater in the Dead Sea. It has 7 times more salt than any other body of water in the world, and it's easy to get salt poisoning if even a small amount of water is ingested.

All the beaches have changing rooms, restrooms, showers, and bathrooms. All have great places to eat at and shop. The northern beaches have gift shops, while the southern

Dead Sea Beach

beaches have access to gift shops, but they're not always right at the resorts.

1. Kalia Beach – Less waves, cheaper entrance fee.
2. Biankini Beach
3. Neve Midbar
4. Ein Gedi Hot Springs – More expensive entrance fees, natural hot mineral springs.

Southern Beaches

The southern beaches have a higher concentration of salt, are more turquoise in color, have more transparent water, are more gradual with fewer waves, are smoother, and are free as they are public beaches.

1. Ein Bokek Public Beach
2. Zohar Public Beach

3. Segregated Public Beach – This beach separates the men from the women for Jewish reasons.

Ekron (Tel Makna Akron)

Ekron is located about 20 miles (32 km.) east of Ashdod and the Mediterranean Sea.

Ekron is the northernmost of the 5 main cities of the Philistines, all located in the coastal plain along the Mediterranean Sea.

Joshua and the Israelites failed to conquer Ekron in the conquest of the Promised Land (Josh. 13:3). It was allotted to Judah in the division of the land and then to the tribe of Dan (Josh. 15:11, 45–46, 19:43). However, Dan moved to the northern part of Israel, and Judah wound up conquering Ekron and inhabiting it (Judg. 1:18).

Tel Ekron

When the Philistines captured the Ark of the Covenant, it was the people of Ekron who proposed to have it sent back to Israel (1 Sam. 5:10, 6:16–17). The Ark went up the valley to Beth-Shemesh, where the Israelites received it with joy (1 Sam. 6:9–18).

After David killed Goliath in the Valley of Elah, the Israelites pursued and defeated the Philistines all the way to Ekron.

Ekron seems to have been the center of worship to the false god Baalzebub. This is seen in the account of the sickness and death of King Ahaziah (2 Kings 1:2–3, 6:16).

Ekron is included, among other cities, in pronouncements of judgment by the prophets Amos 1:8, Jeremiah 25:20, Zephaniah 2:4, and Zechariah 9:5–7.

Gath (Tell es Safi)

Biblical Gath (known today as Tell es-Safi, is 14 miles (23 km.) east of Ashdod and Ashkelon, which are close to the Mediterranean Sea.

Gath was one of the five main cities of the Philistines (Josh. 13:3; 1 Sam. 6:17).

Tel Gath

It was a well-fortified walled city (2 Chron. 26:6).

Joshua and the Israelites were unable to conquer Gath despite the numerous conflicts between the Israelites and the inhabitants of Gath.

It wasn't until King David that the city was conquered and became part of the Israelite Kingdom (1 Chron. 18:1).

Its name is most remembered as the home of the giant, Goliath, whom David slew (1 Sam. 17:4).

The people of Ashdod took the Ark of the Covenant to Gath when they were smitten with tumors from God. Later, the people of Gath were smitten as well with tumors and took the ark to Ekron (1 Sam. 5:8–10).

David sought refuge in Gath on two occasions when King Saul was seeking his life (1 Sam. 21:10, 27:2–4).

Gath appears to have been destroyed after being taken by David because Rehoboam restored it under his reign (2 Chron. 11:8).

Later, the Philistines regained control of Gath, for we see that King Uzziah conquered it and destroyed its walls (2 Chron. 26:6).

Once again, it must have been restored and rebuilt because Hazael, of Damascus, captured it once more (2 Kings 12:17).

During the time of the prophet Amos, Gath seems to have been destroyed (Amos 6:2), and is only mentioned in Micah 1:10, as a proverb, *"Tell it not in Gath."*

Since the time Gath was destroyed, most likely in the middle of the 8th century BC, it has laid desolate.

Gaza

Gaza is one of the 5 main cities of the Philistines and seems to be the oldest of them all.

It's a coastal city on the Mediterranean Sea about 40 miles (64 km.) south of Joppa (Jaffa). Gaza was also located on the Via Maris.

Gaza was on a hill rising about 200 ft. (61 m.) above the valley floor. There were sand dunes between it and the sea, which was about 2 miles away.

Gaza ruins 1898 (American Colony or Matson photo service, Library of Congress)

In the conquest of the Promised Land, Joshua and the Israelites failed to conquer Gaza, along with several other main cities of the Philistines (Josh. 10:41, 11:22).

Later, the tribe of Judah captured Gaza but couldn't control it for long, and it fell back into the hands of the Philistines (Judg. 1:18).

During the time of Samson, it was the heavy gates of Gaza that Samson carried all the way up to Hebron (Judg. 16:1-3).

After the Philistines defeated the Israelites in battle and captured the Ark of the Covenant during the priesthood of Eli and his two wicked sons, Gaza, along with the other main cities of the Philistines, sent a trespass offering to God when the ark was returned to the Israelites at Beth-Shemesh (1 Sam. 6:17-18).

When Hezekiah reigned, he defeated and pursued the Philistines to Gaza but did not seem to have captured the city. However, the Assyrians later captured it in 720 BC.

In the New Testament, Philip was sent to Gaza to evangelize the

Ethiopian eunuch (Acts 8:26).

Today, because ancient Gaza lies in the Gaza Strip, where land is scarce and Israeli interests are not valued, the remains of ancient Gaza are practically nonexistent.

Ziklag

While the exact location of biblical Ziklag is debated, most archaeologists now place it at Tel Ser'a (Tel esh-Shariah), which is in the southernmost area of Judea about 14 miles (23 km.) northwest of Tel Beer Sheba and about 15 miles (24 km.) east of Gaza.

Ziklag is first mentioned in the Bible as part of the inheritance of the tribe of Judah (Josh. 15:31). It was allotted to the tribe of Simeon (within the tribe of Judah), but the Israelites apparently failed to conquer it because Ziklag was still under Philistine control when Saul reigned as king (Josh. 19:5).

Because for many years King Saul sought to harm David, David fled to Ziklag seeking refuge after the death of Samuel. As a result, he lived in Ziklag with six hundred men and their households in Philistine territory.

While living in Ziklag, David petitioned Achish, the Philistine king of Gath, to give him the city of Ziklag (1 Sam. 27:5–6). Achish consented and gave Ziklag to David.

During David's rule over Ziklag, which lasted 16 months, he made it his military home base. From Ziklag, David raided many of the cities of the Amalekites. Because many soldiers from Israel were disappointed with Saul's leadership, they joined forces with David's private army during this time (1 Chron. 12:1–22). When war broke out between the Philistines and Israel during the reign of King Saul, David and his small army attempted to join the Philistine army to fight against Saul.

However, the Philistine leaders rejected David and sent him away from the battle. While David and the Philistines were away, the Amalekites attacked Ziklag. They burned the city and took captive all the women, children, and the elderly.

When David and his men returned to Ziklag, they found it had been destroyed by fire, and their families had been taken captive (1 Sam. 30:1–3). In response, David and his army pursued the Amalekites and recovered their families and possessions. (1 Sam. 30:16–31).

While David was living in Ziklag, he received the news of the defeat of Israel by the Philistines and Saul and Jonathan's deaths (2 Samuel 4:10).

Ziklag remained in control of Israel from this point on and is last mentioned in the Bible as one of the cities the Jews inhabited after returning from exile in Babylon (Neh. 11:28).

Timeline of Israel

Negev & Southern Israel Biblical Sites Guide

Why it's so important to understand a brief overview of the historical periods of Israel.

The Holy Land is an old place, about the oldest in the world! While in the Holy Land, you'll be seeing things as old as 6,000 years. That's old! Different periods of history will be referred to when describing Israel's holy sites and places. Please realize that there will likely be several key events at a particular site that have taken place there. Each event will have happened during a specific period in Israel's history. If you can understand the different periods a little, you'll get much more out of your experience.

Chronology of Time Used by Archaeologist and Historians
- Early Bronze Age   4000–2000 BC
- Middle Bronze Age   2000–1500 BC
- Late Bronze Age   1500–1200 BC
- Iron 1 Age   1200–1000 BC
- Iron 2 Age   1000–586 BC

Canaanite Period   4000–1875 BC
- 4000 BC – Canaanites inhabit the land of Israel.
- 2500 BC – Noah and the Great Flood.
- 2100 BC – Tower of Babel
- 2095 BC – Abraham moves to the land of Canaan from Ur of the Chaldeans.
- 1880 BC – Jacob and his family move to Egypt to live with Joseph.

Israelite Period   1450–965 BC
- 1450 BC – Exodus of the Israelites from Egypt.
- 1406 BC – Jews enter the Promised Land.
- 1012 BC – Saul unifies the 12 Hebrew tribes into the United Kingdom of Israel.
- 1010–970 BC – David's reign.

First Temple Period   970–586 BC
- 970–925 BC – Solomon's reign; glory years of the Kingdom of Israel.
- 950 BC – Solomon builds the magnificent temple on Mount

Timeline of Israel

  Moriah in Jerusalem (same place Abraham intended to sacrifice Isaac).
- 926 BC – Kingdom of Israel divides because of Solomon's sins. Jeroboam reigns over the northern Kingdom of Israel from Samaria. Rehoboam reigns over the southern Kingdom of Israel from Jerusalem.
- 722 BC – Assyrians conquer and deport most of the northern Kingdom of Israel to Assyria.
- 586 BC – Babylonians conquer Jerusalem and Judah under Nebuchadnezzar and deport most of the southern Kingdom of Judah to Babylon.

Second Temple Period   535–444 BC

- 535 BC – Many Jews return from Babylonia; Second Temple began to be rebuilt.
- 458 BC – Ezra returns to Jerusalem with second wave of Jews to continue rebuilding the Second Temple.
- 444 BC – Nehemiah returns to Jerusalem to rebuild the city walls.

Hellenistic Period (Greek Rule)   333–167 BC

- 333 BC – Alexander the Great defeats the Persian Empire and sets out to conquer the world. After his sudden death in 323 BC, the Greek Empire is divided. During this period the Bible is translated into Greek (the Septuagint).

Hasmonean Period (Maccabean Rule)   167–63 BC

- 167 BC – When the Jews were prohibited from practicing Judaism, and their temple was desecrated as part of an effort to impose Greek-oriented culture and customs on the entire population, the Jews revolted. First led by Mattathias of the priestly Hasmonean family and then by his son Judah the Maccabee, the Jews subsequently entered Jerusalem and purified the temple. This purification of the temple is remembered by the Jewish Holiday, Hanukkah (164 BC).

Roman Period (Roman Rule)   63 BC–330 AD

- 63 BC – Jerusalem is captured by Roman general Pompey.
- 37 BC–4 BC – Herod, Roman vassal king, rules the Land of Israel. He enlarges the Temple Mount and rebuilds the temple. He also

builds other monumental projects, including Caesarea, Herodian, Cave of the Patriarchs, and Masada.

- 4 BC – Jesus is born in Bethlehem.
- 27–30 AD – Ministry of Jesus.
- 30 AD – Jesus crucified.
- 66 AD – Jewish revolt against the Romans.
- 70 AD – Destruction of Jerusalem and Second Temple.
- 74 AD – Fall of Masada.
- 132 AD – Bar Kokhba Revolt. Roman Emperor Hadrian destroys Jerusalem and builds Aelia Capitolina, a pagan city in its place. Many holy sites are preserved, but with pagan shrines on them.

Byzantine Period (Eastern Roman Empire Rule) 330–614 AD

- 313 – Emperor Constantine recognizes Christianity, later becoming a Christian himself.
- 326 – Constantine's mother, Helena, goes to the Holy Land and builds many churches and basilicas on holy sites.

Persian Period 614–628 AD

- 614 – Persian conquest of the Holy Land. Many churches and monasteries destroyed.

Byzantine Period Reestablished 628–638 AD

- 628 – Holy Land recaptured by the Byzantines.

Muslim/Arab Period 638–1099 AD

- 638 – Muslim/Arab conquest of the Holy Land completed. Rule is by Caliphs from Damascus, then from Baghdad, and then Egypt.
- 691 – On top of the First and Second Temples in Jerusalem, the Dome of the Rock is built by Caliph Abd el-Malik.

Crusader Period 1099–1291 AD

- 1099 – Crusaders (Catholic armies from Rome) conquer Jerusalem and many parts of Israel.
- 1147 – Second Crusade arrives in the Holy Land.
- 1187 – Destruction of the Crusader army by Muslim leader Saladin. Collapse of Crusader Kingdom begins.

Timeline of Israel

- 1265 – Mamelukes, led by Sultan Beybars, conquer the Holy Land.
- 1270 – Final Crusade arrives, and all its participants massacred.
- 1291 – Last Crusader stronghold of Acco taken, ending Crusader rule.

Mamluk (Muslim) Period   1291–1517 AD

- 1291 – Mamluk rule begins.
- 1333 – Franciscan Order established in Jerusalem. Its members care for holy places and pilgrims.
- By the end of the Middle Ages, the country's urban centers were virtually in ruins, most of Jerusalem was abandoned, and the small Jewish community was poverty-stricken. The period of Mamluk decline was darkened by political and economic upheavals, plagues, locust invasions, and devastating earthquakes.

Ottoman (Muslim) Period   1517–1917 AD

- 1517 – Following the Ottoman conquest in 1517, the land was divided into four districts and attached administratively to the province of Damascus and ruled from Istanbul.
- 1520 – Suleiman the Magnificent rebuilds the city walls of Jerusalem.
- 1799 – Napoleon Bonaparte invades Israel but fails to capture it and is forced to leave.
- 1860 – The first neighborhood, Mishkenot Sha'ananim, is built outside of Jerusalem's city walls.
- 1882 – First large-scale immigration to Israel, mainly from Russia.
- 1904 – Second large-scale immigration from Russia and Poland.

British Period   1917–1948 AD

- 1917 – British Foreign Minister Lord Balfour issued on November 2, 1917, the so-called Balfour Declaration, which gave official support for the "establishment in Israel of a national home for the Jewish people" with the commitment not to be prejudiced against the rights of the non-Jewish communities.
- 1947 – The United Nations approved the partition of Israel into separate Jewish and Arab states on November 29, 1947.

Negev & Southern Israel Biblical Sites Guide

State of Israel Period   1948 to Present

- 1948 – On the day when the British Mandate in Palestine expired, the State of Israel was instituted on May 14, 1948, by the Jewish National Council under the presidency of David Ben Gurion.
- 1948–1949 – The Arab-Israeli War; the Arabs refused to accept the newly established State of Israel. Egypt, Syria, Transjordan, Lebanon, and Iraq attack Israel, but within a year, Israel defeated its attackers.
- 1950 – Western Jerusalem was proclaimed the capital city of Israel on January 23, 1950.
- 1956 – The Suez Crisis: Israelis invade Egyptian territory in October of 1956.
- 1956 – After Egyptian President Gamal Abdel Nasser nationalized the company which administered the Suez Canal, a joint attack by the French and British was launched. Egypt suffered military disaster on November 2, 1956. Israel captured the Sinai Peninsula, but after international condemnation, Israel was forced to withdraw.
- 1967 – Six-Day War: after Egypt closed the Straits of Tiran on May 22, 1967, Israel launched an attack on Egyptian, Jordanian, Syrian, and Iraqi airports on June 5, 1967. After six days, Israel conquered Jerusalem, the Golan Heights, Sinai, and the West Bank.
- 1973 – Yom Kippur War: on October 6, 1973, on the Jewish holiday of Yom Kippur, Syria and Egypt launched a surprise attack against Israel. After initial success of the attackers, Israel managed to cross the Suez into Egypt and endangered Cairo. After the intervention of the USA and USSR, military operations ended on October 25, 1973.
- 1978 – The Camp David Accord was signed by Israeli Prime Minister Menahen Begin, and Egyptian President Anvar as Sadat in September 1978, in Camp David, USA. Israel agreed to withdraw from the occupied Sinai Peninsula.
- 1979 – The Israel-Egypt Peace Treaty was signed on March 26, 1979, in Washington.

Maps of Israel

Negev & Southern Israel Biblical Sites Guide

Twelve Tribes of Israel

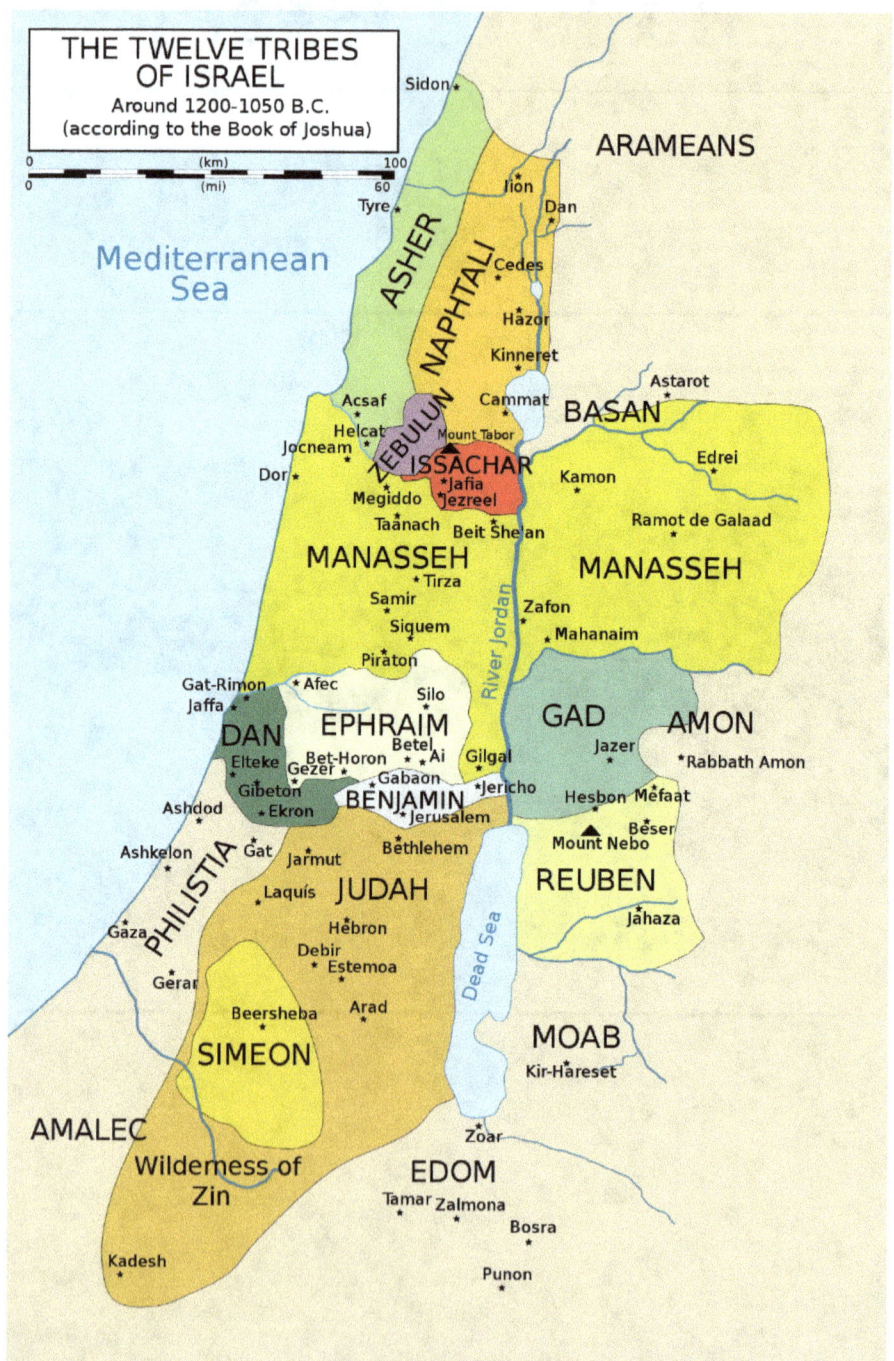

Maps of Israel

Divided Kingdom

Regions of Israel

Maps of Israel

Israel Today

Travel Orientation

Travel Orientation

Understanding the Holy Sites in Israel

The Need to Understand What You're Going to See

It would be wonderful if the Holy Land was exactly the same as it was 2,000 years ago when Christ walked its paths, or 4,000 years ago when Abraham traversed its hillsides and valleys. However, 4,000 years is a long time, and there have been many changes that have taken place during this time span. It's hard for us to understand, but 4,000 or even 2,000 years is a long time! Because of its strategic location in the world, no other country has had as many kingdoms occupy it or as many battles fought on its soil as Israel. This, along with time, has led to much change to Israel and its holy sites.

The good news is that many of the biblical sites are in their natural state and appear much the same as they did when the events that happened there occurred. Other sites have had monuments, churches, or basilicas built near, or on them, and are not exactly as they appeared when the events that occurred there happened. Also, many sites have had many events happen in one spot over thousands of years, so it would be impossible to have each event preserved just the way it happened.

Understanding What Some of The Holy Sites Will Be Like

Many of these monuments, churches, or basilicas will have a Catholic, Arabic, or Mid-Eastern look. They're very different from what we're accustomed to seeing, and at first glance, you might find this unattractive. You also might disagree with the religious backgrounds of some of these sites and feel somewhat uncomfortable as well. In addition, you most likely will find other people visiting the Holy Land from other countries who are actually worshiping and kissing some of the adornments on these sites. On a previous trip to Israel, some in our group found all this a little repulsive and chose not to enter some of these holy sites. Because of these possible negative reactions, we would like to provide you with a little background and history about how these holy sites have been preserved so your sightseeing experience can be the best as possible during your time in the Holy Land.

Negev & Southern Israel Biblical Sites Guide

A Little History

Even before the time of Christ and afterward, many of the holy sites were marked out and preserved. Then, about 300 years after the time of Christ, the Roman Empire (world power at that time) embraced Christianity. At that time, the mother of Emperor Constantine (Helena) was one of the first of the royal family to convert to Christianity. Later, Emperor Constantine did as well. Helena came to the Holy Land and wanted to preserve some of the holy sites, so she had churches, monuments, and basilicas built over some of the key holy places. These included the Church of the Holy Sepulture, Church of the Nativity, Basilica in the Garden of Gethsemane, Church of the Annunciation, and others. Helena, and others throughout history, felt such emotion and awe at these holy sites that they wanted to honor and preserve them for future generations. The Early Church during this period was the first to be in charge of these sites, and then because the Early Church slowly evolved into what we know as the Catholic Church, many of these holy sites came under the care of the Catholic Church. The monuments, churches, and basilicas were not always Catholic in nature, so we shouldn't assume that they shared the same religious views at their inception.

There were others as well that came to the Holy Land to build churches, monuments, and basilicas on these holy sites (Eastern Orthodox Church, Armenians, Russians, Greeks, etc.). Their hearts felt the same awe and emotion as others who came, so they too built on or by these holy sites to honor and preserve them.

Some of these holy sites are ancient (from as old as 5,000 years), and the churches have a Mid-Eastern style look.

Gratefulness to Those Who Preserved the Biblical Sites

If it hadn't been for those who built monuments or churches on or by the holy sites, they would have had other buildings, roads, and infrastructure built over them and lost to the world forever. These early pilgrims felt the same awe and emotion you will feel, and we certainly can't fault them for this.

Because of all the adornments and construction over the centuries, it's hard to imagine how some of these sites would have looked in their original setting. However, the years of activity and tradition at these holy sites give greater weight to their authenticity. And while we might disagree with the decorations, atmosphere of these places, and religious backgrounds, we can certainly appreciate and admire all the devotion and sacrifice made to preserve them.

Some Might Find These Churches, Monuments, and Basilicas Repulsive

Part of the reason some might find the places they see in Israel as repulsive will have to do with a difference in religious faith. Another reason is due to a misunderstanding of style. These holy sites have a very different style than what we're accustomed to in modern churches. Most of the oldest churches we see today in our own countries are just a few hundred years old and have somewhat the same architecture and style from our modern era. As a result, we're just not used to seeing churches close to 1,500 years old, and older.

Closing Thoughts

1. Entering these churches, monuments, and basilicas to see these holy sites doesn't mean we're in any way embracing and accepting their religious beliefs.

2. While the style, religious background, and adornments might not be to our taste, the motives of those who preserved these sites seem to be noble and honorable. As you see these sites, you will understand why these early pilgrims wanted to preserve them.

3. It's important to note that we, from a modern mindset, have a different view and taste regarding building styles. Because to us, something 200-400 years old seems really ancient, we need to realize that seeing something 1,500 years old has an entirely different architectural look and sense to it than what we're accustomed to seeing.

Hopefully, this info will help you. As mentioned, on a previous trip to Israel, some didn't really understand these things beforehand, and it took them a bit to get themselves wrapped around some of these concepts. It was kind of a self-discovery process. For this reason, this orientation and background are provided so you can get the most out of your Holy Land Experience and not get bogged down in this area.

How to Get the Most Out of Your Holy Land Trip

How to See What Many Don't See in the Holy Land

Understand that half of what there is to see in the Holy Land is hidden from most that walk her paths. They are unseen spiritual truths, only revealed to the sensitive and spiritual of heart. Try to get as close to God as you can prior, and during your time in the Holy Land, so you can see and hear things that many don't see during their visit there. The Holy Land is not just places and historical artifacts; it's an experience — an experience that is spiritual in nature and eye-opening for those who can see in this realm.

You Won't Be Able to See Everything

It would be great to see every detail at every holy site, but that would take months, if not years, to do. It's important to understand that there is a lot to see and, therefore, just the highlights can be seen. You'll be eating the frosting off the cake and won't be able to eat the whole thing. As a result, please don't be discouraged if you can't spend as much time in each place as you'd wish. You'll have to move along to see just the highlights, and if you stay too long at one place, that means you'll be saying "No" to another.

Your Trip Won't be Perfect

It would be wonderful if you could be guaranteed a perfect trip with a perfect experience, but that's just not reality. Going to the Holy Land is undoubtedly the closest you'll get to the "Trip of a Lifetime," but please don't get your hopes up so high that you're let down and feel discouraged if it doesn't turn out as you dreamed. Your trip won't be perfect. Your leader and the rest in your group will probably not live up to your expectations either. The only perfect person on the trip will be you (well, maybe not exactly perfect, but pretty close to it, lol). So just prepare yourself to understand that things just aren't going to be flawless.

Trust God for Your Experience

It's also easy to have preconceived ideas of what to expect; the emotions you're going to feel, the dreams you might have of the Holy Land, and the experience you want to have. Please try to set some of

Travel Orientation

these aside and trust God to give you the experience He has for you. Don't get everything built up so high that it would be impossible to fulfill them. Trust God to bless you and teach you what He has for you. He's the One who's worked everything out for you to go, and I'm certain He has special things to teach you. Trust in Him and be looking for what He has for you. And after everything is said and done, be content with what He gives you.

Negev & Southern Israel Biblical Sites Guide

Understanding Group Travel Dynamics

Traveling with Others

Part of the joy and richness of your Holy Land Experience will come from sharing it with others. Going somewhere alone is never as much fun as doing it with someone else. The impact and fullness of the experience will come alive as it's experienced as a group rather than as an individual or couple. For this reason, you'll want to consider a few things to make your Holy Land Experience the best as possible.

Try to Think as a Group and Not as an Individual

Traveling as a group is very different from traveling as an individual or couple. There will be other team members in your group, and each person needs to realize they're part of a larger event than just themselves. The whole team will be depending on others to be punctual, courteous, thoughtful, and pleasant. Try to take into consideration that what you do affects everyone else on the team.

Try to Keep Up with the Group

It will be important that you keep up with the group and not linger too long seeing things during your travels. Each day it is wise to appoint a "Follow-up Person" who'll bring up the group's rear and make sure everyone stays together. Because you'll be seeing some really interesting things, it will be easy to get lost in these and forget that there are other things to see as well.

Try to Be Punctual

Everything from wake-up times, mealtimes, arrival times, departure times, and the site-seeing schedule for each day needs to be considered. Because you are spending a lot of money and taking precious time out of your busy life to experience the Holy Land, you'll want to be as punctual as possible so you and your team can see everything as planned. Your group can only be as fast as the slowest person, so try to be punctual and thoughtful of others. If you tend to be a late person, consider getting a head start on things by starting earlier than normal so you can be on time.

Travel Orientation

Try to Be Patient and Courteous

Be aware that sometime during the trip, you'll likely feel tired, a bit irritated with others, or upset at something that's happened. Do your best to overlook the faults of others and try to keep yourself in check. Also, realize that we have an enemy who will do his best to take away from our experience by using others or problems. Be alert and prayerful! Keep yourself close to God and do your best to love others and take everything in stride.

Try to Be Rested Up Before Your Holy Land Trip

Because you're going to be expending a lot of energy during the trip, try to get as rested as possible before departure. To illustrate this point, we'll use the term "gauges" to help us out. We all know that most of our vehicles have gauges: gas gauge, temperature gauge, oil gauge, etc. Using this analogy for our bodies, we all have bodily gauges as well. We have physical, emotional, mental, and spiritual gauges. Before your trip, try to get your bodily gauges as full as possible. By doing so, you'll get more out of your trip and be more joyful and patient with others.

Tips for filling up your bodily gauges before trip departure:

- Try and scale down on your activities and output before the trip. For example, cut back on meetings, outings, get-togethers, and social events.
- Get plenty of sleep.
- Get plenty of exercise (you'll be doing quite a bit of walking, so try to get in walking shape before the trip).
- Get as much of your responsibilities and commitments done ahead of time, and don't wait until the last minute to take care of things. There will be plenty of last-minute things to do, so don't add to them by procrastinating.
- Try to get packed and ready at your earliest convenience. If you need to shop for trip items, try to do so plenty of time in advance.

By taking into consideration these tips, you'll start your trip with your bodily gauges full and not empty. And when you think about it, who would start a long journey with their car having an empty gas tank and little or no oil in the engine?

Travel Tips for Israel

1. Get in shape physically before you go to Israel. You will be doing a lot of walking, so the better shape you're in, the easier and more pleasant your time will be. At least a month before your trip, start walking at least 15-30 minutes a day.
2. Activate your credit/debit cards before departure to Israel.
3. Make sure your Passport is up to date and valid. It must have at least 6 months before expiration from your last day in Israel to be valid.
4. Don't shave your body before taking a dip in the Dead Sea. The salt and minerals will irritate your skin.
5. Don't show public affection with the opposite sex, especially on the Temple Mount and Muslim sites.
6. Don't be afraid to bargain for purchases at marketplaces. It's expected, so take part in it.
7. Establish meeting places at each site so that if for some reason you get lost or separated, you can find each other.
8. Carry a water bottle and stay hydrated.
9. Pack layered types of clothing instead of heavy clothes.
10. Carry your personal items in a safe place on your person.
11. Take a good camera or video camera.
12. Get used to people smoking as it's very common in Israel and the Middle East.
13. Many Israelis are not religious but secular. This might seem strange, but it's true.
14. Carry a copy of your Passport.
15. Women should dress very modestly, especially when visiting holy sites.
16. Men should wear hats when visiting Jewish holy sites.
17. Men should not wear hats when visiting Christian holy sites.

Travel Orientation

Packing List

Clothes

Dressing in layers is best when considering your clothes. For the most part, the weather will be warm and sunny during the summer and cooler in the winter. Following are some suggested items that might be helpful:

- Casual pants for hiking and sightseeing (casual can be worn the whole trip).
- Nicer shorts are okay at many places. However, at some sites like the Temple Mount, Western Wall, etc., pants are recommended. Also, for women, being very modest is recommended at these sites as well.
- Casual long sleeve shirts
- Short sleeve shirts
- Bathing suit (for the Dead Sea if you want to take a dip)
- 2 Plastic bags for wet clothes.
- Undergarments
- Socks
- Light jacket
- Sturdy walking shoes with traction for many stone paths and roads you'll traverse. FYI- many of the streets are paved with stone, and it's challenging to wear shoes with awkward heels/soles on uneven pavement.
- Sleepwear
- Hat for sun protection purposes.
- Men will need to wear a hat or equivalent on their heads when entering Jewish sites and synagogues.
- Ladies will need a shawl or equivalent when entering Muslim areas.

General Items

- Slimline travel Bible
- Small notebook and pen for taking notes
- Travel alarm
- Flashlight (mini) or cell phone with flashlight

Negev & Southern Israel Biblical Sites Guide

- Camera/video camera
- Film or storage disks for your camera (bring plenty, because they're much more expensive in Israel)
- Daypack/backpack (can be used as an airplane carry-on and for travel in Israel).
- Ziplock bags for lunches and for putting the relics in you might gather along the way in Israel.
- Umbrella – small contractible type
- Sunglasses
- Plug adapter for plugging devices into the outlets in Israel.

  Note: The outlets in Israel are different than the states. You'll need this adapter for plugging things in to be charged, etc.

- Charger converter needed for Israel (needed for charging cameras, etc.) Note: Electricity in Israel is 220 volts. In America, and many other countries, it's 110 volts. Many electronic devices today can adapt to both voltages. However, if you plan to take an item that cannot use 220 volts, you will need a converter.

Personal Items

- Toothbrush
- Toothpaste
- Deodorant
- Lip balm
- Razor
- After-shave
- Band-Aids
- Feminine items
- Sunscreen
- Tylenol/Ibuprofen
- Eyeglasses/contact lenses
- Prescription medicines

Travel Orientation

Documents & Items to Carry with You at all Times

There are several options for carrying your money and important documents with you on your trip. For example, you can use a money belt (waist style or necklace style) or pockets on your pants or shirt that can be buttoned and are secure.

- Passport – Must have 6 months left before expiring from the dates of your trip.
- Copy of your Passport
- Driver's License
- Cash
- Credit/Debit Card (make sure to activate your cards for Israel or international travel).

    Note: It's handy to use your debit card for drawing out Shekels for spending money in Israel. You'll also get the best exchange rate by using it as well.

- Travel Visa received in Israel at customs.

    Special Note: When arriving in Israel, you'll go through customs to receive your visa for your stay in Israel. It will be a small piece of paper. ***Please don't lose it!*** You will need it on several occasions while in the country. You can tuck it away in your Passport if you'd like.

About the Author

Todd M. Fink is the founder and director of Go Missions to Mexico and Holy Land Site Ministries. He holds the following degrees: Bachelor of Theology from Freelandia Bible College, Master of Divinity studies at Western Seminary, Master of Theology from Freedom Bible College and Seminary, Master of Divinity from Trinity Theological Seminary, and a Ph.D. in theology from Trinity Theological Seminary.

He served as youth/associate pastor for 11 years at an Evangelical church in Oregon (1987–1998).

Todd is currently serving as pastor and missionary with Go Missions to Mexico Ministries in Mexico (1998–present).

He also is serving with Holy Land Site ministries and has a passion for the Holy Land. He has developed a large website and YouTube channel with videos and teachings about almost every site in Israel. In addition, he leads tour trips to Israel and has written books about the Holy Land.

Todd is an author, speaker, and teacher. He has a deep passion for God's Word and enjoys helping people understand its eternal truths.

He is married to his lovely wife, Letsy, and has four grown children.

Books by Todd M. Fink

Israel Biblical Sites Travel Guide

Israel Biblical Sites Bible Companion

Jerusalem & Central Israel Biblical Sites Guide

Sea of Galilee & Northern Israel Biblical Sites Guide

Negev & Southern Israel Biblical Sites Guide

Biblical Discipleship: Essential Components for Reaching Spiritual Maturity

Biblical Discipleship: Essential Components for Reaching Spiritual Maturity 16 Week Study Guide

What is the Gospel and How to Share It

Discovering the True Riches of Life

A Biblical Analysis of Corrective Church Discipline

Discipulado Bíblico

Discipulado Bíblico Guía de Estudio

Please visit: ToddMichaelFink.com to see or purchase books.

Connect with Todd

Email: holylandsite.com@gmail.com

Facebook: Todd Mike Fink

Facebook Ministry Page: Holy Land Site

YouTube Channel: Holy Land Site

Websites:

HolyLandSite.com

ToddMichaelFink.com

SelahBookPress.com

GoMissionsToMexico.com

MinisteriosCasaDeLuz.com

www.ingramcontent.com/pod-product-compliance
Lightning Source LLC
Chambersburg PA
CBHW062037120526
44592CB00035B/1205